Photography by Diana M. Lott

from **We** to **Me**

emerging **self** after divorce

best-selling book by award-winning author

Kerri Hummingbird Sami

First published in the United States of America by Siwarkinte Publishing

From We To Me: Emerging Self After Divorce
Kerri Hummingbird Sami

Cover design by © Kerri Hummingbird Sami
Photograph of Kerri Hummingbird Sami by Diana M. Lott Photography.
www.dianamlottphotography.com

This book may be ordered directly from Amazon.com.

ISBN-13: 978-0692551738
ISBN-10: 0692551735

For more information about Kerri Hummingbird, visit:
Web: www.kerrihummingbird.com
Twitter: @KerriHummingbrd
Facebook: Kerri.Hummingbird
Pinterest: kerrihummingbrd
YouTube: Kerri Hummingbird
Instagram: kerri.hummingbird

The caterpillar doesn't know it's becoming a butterfly. It thinks it's dying.

♥

"If you take your happiness and put it in someone's hands, sooner or later, she is going to break it. If you give your happiness to someone else, she can always take it away. Then if happiness can only come from inside of you and is the result of your love, you are responsible for your happiness."

— *don Miguel Ruiz*

Acknowledgements

I thank my sons, Garrett and Tanner, for remaining by my side on my journey from We to Me. I thank my parents for supporting my growth into a woman and mother. I thank my former partner of 20 years for being my biggest teacher and helping to catalyze my journey of self-discovery. I thank my mentors for the beautiful teachings that guided me externally on what was, essentially, a vulnerable inwards exploration. And I thank every man I dated for teaching me about myself through the mirror of relationship.

Most of all, I thank myself for holding the faith that a butterfly would emerge from my toxic cocoon.

♥

If you are currently in a situation where your safety is threatened, please consult with legal and protective resources immediately. The content of this book is primarily designed for divorce situations that do not involve domestic abuse.

Intent

I started this book with the intent that when it was finished, I would have arrived at the place I wanted to be: 'Me.' Writing this book became my way of processing the end of my 20 year relationship, and understanding the uncomfortable twists and turns my life was taking as a single person. I needed to digest the painful moments that pushed me out of my comfort zone and make some sense out of them. Through writing, I explored my beliefs and behaviors with a high degree of awareness that shined the light on places I needed to do something *different* to get to where I wanted to be. Setting intent to share with you what I discovered along my journey from 'We' to 'Me' mandated that I first slog through the lessons myself, and deeply feel the shifts in thought and deed so that I could articulate them.

What I feel I have uncovered are some structural cracks in the foundation of our society's beliefs around relationship, and how people interrelate as a 'couple.' I spent all of my life immersed in a relationship model I was domesticated to believe was the way to be 'complete': find another person to commit to love me *forever*. When I rebelliously left my marriage and began the healing process, I thought I was preparing myself for another, better, couple relationship. But what I ended up learning sent me in a very different direction.

As I have digested wisdom from my mentors and spiritual thought leaders, I have discovered for myself what they already taught thousands: love begins with self. Each of us comes into life with a primary directive—to grow and expand our being through our experiences. Growth and expansion are often accelerated by being in intimate relationship with another person. But what our society got backwards was putting the 'We' in front of the 'Me,' or worse, in *place* of 'Me.' So often we believe the source of love comes from a 'We' relationship, and therefore we are reluctant to do anything that disrupts the 'We' for fear of losing the love we rely on to feel good. We also got the message that the 'We' relationship has to last forever.

This kind of 'We' thinking slows or stops exploration and learning necessary for 'Me' to grow and fulfill the life mission each of us came here to accomplish.

The alternative I have found for myself is to stand fearlessly in the power of 'Me,' honoring the truth that I am on a solo journey through life, even if I am engaged in intimate relationships and surrounded by family and friends. I am the only being inside of 'Me,' the only consciousness guiding my moment-by-moment choices, and the only person completely dependent on my existence. I came into this life alone, and I will leave it alone, and in the middle I will enjoy many fulfilling 'We' relationships that teach me what I need to know about 'Me.'

♥

Table of Contents

At the end, there is a beginning

ଓ A caterpillar doesn't know it's becoming a butterfly.
It thinks it's dying. ଓ

The end of a significant long-term relationship also marks the beginning of a new phase of your life. At the ending, however, our thoughts tend to be focused backwards on the past that leads up to the present moment of heartbreak and disintegration of all we came to hold dear. There is one constant in this world and that is *change*, and yet as humans we do everything in our power to prevent change once we land in a spot that feels good. So when that feel-good spot comes to closure, it is usually long past the moment that it actually stopped feeling good because we tend to lie to ourselves to prolong the illusion of feeling good so we don't have to change.

Compounding the resistance to change is the big promise that we made at the start of the relationship which is usually along the lines of "til death do us part." Having to admit that human frailty won out over impossible vows is tantamount to admitting failure at being a person of your word. And if your journey through life included your parents divorcing as a child, and the child self living inside of you vowed to never do that to your children, well then you're in a pickle when you realize this marriage is done. Kaput.

In the confusion of the end our minds can grasp for explanations, seeking that critical moment that, had we just known its importance and done something differently, we might still be in the relationship and maintained our big promise and our feelings of self-worth. To save us from our own worst judge (ourselves), we can become angry and want to blame someone (easy target= ex-spouse) for creating the situation that is now leading to *change*.

The truth is, this relationship is ending and a new phase of your life is beginning and in the middle space is an incredible period of total disintegration of everything you knew to be 'you' and 'your life' and it feels a lot like what it must feel like to be in a cocoon...not caterpillar anymore, and not yet butterfly. Imaginal soup. The

7

greatest transformation is possible in this uncomfortable and disorienting space. Don't be too quick to 'become' the new you; hang out in discomfort and let the butterfly you already are unfold and surprise you.

As you gain distance from your relationship, the gift is that you can understand what you learned from it and incorporate that wisdom into your way of living henceforth. The gift of the disintegration period is that you can liberate yourself from all the outmoded constructs that no longer apply to you because you have changed, and by releasing these constructs (subconscious and learned beliefs about relationships) you can invite wondrous new possibilities. With some time and perspective you can really see how different you are now than you were when you met your former spouse, and this can serve as a marker of your transformation.

℃

Many events of my past are now simply stories that I tell to teach and inspire and to reframe again (and again) what I think actually happened from my new vantage point of time and perspective. I am fascinated by the human experience and the stories we tell to try to capture it and make sense of it. So here is the story of the ending of my marriage, as I have decided to tell it today.

The last two years of my marriage were mayhem, and in retrospect, I understand why. My cocoon had grown too tight and was suffocating me. There was a 'Me' longing to be born, to spread her wings, and to take flight. Chaos erupted from within me and I was unable to contain it. Shiva took control of me—the Destroyer, the Transformer—and everything I touched fell apart into dust. At the time, I felt I could do nothing right. I felt entirely wrong within the confines of my marriage that I had built with my husband, and felt rage with the roles I had adopted to make the relationship work. I was angry at myself for not being able to stop this destruction, for not being capable of returning quietly and peacefully to the cage I had built for myself over a period of twenty years.

What I didn't understand at the time is that the fires of change do not stop simply because you want to lie down and pretend everything is just fine the way it is. No matter how much alcohol I consumed to numb myself from perceiving the truth, the truth escaped and reared its ugly head, taunting me ceaselessly. Anti-anxiety and anti-depressant medications didn't stop me from plunging further down the rabbit hole of my becoming. There was simply no stopping it.

Shiva was relentless. He wanted the utter destruction of the Self I was claiming to be, of the masks I was wearing to please my world, of the marital contracts I had blindly co-written, and of the delusions I clung to despite the despair they delivered to my doorstep. Crap is still crap, even if it's wrapped up in a pretty pink bow.

I was becoming a person I loathed. False, pretending, fake, full of pretense, beautiful on the outside and rotting on the inside. I hadn't spoken my truth in so long I wasn't sure what the truth was anymore. My throat was clogged with choked-back anger and sadness. I hated the arguments and the endless critical debates that made me question my sanity, and so I submerged my voice under oceans of anger. Self-betrayal was a regular state of being, and the more I denied expression of my truth, the more the internal pressure mounted until I would erupt with rebellious fiery demonstrations of latent power. Escapism and avoidant behaviors became my coping mechanisms. I regularly drifted into fantasy in my mind when physically at home, and fled the coop to art shows as many weekends as I could demand in the name of making a living. While away from home, I did as I pleased with whoever I wanted.

I thought, at the time, that I was betraying my marriage and proving what a horrible person I could be. I didn't know that I was fighting for my soul. I didn't know that Shiva came because I was dying on the inside. I didn't realize that Shiva was ripping apart my cocoon so I could emerge from the toxic sludge and get a breath of fresh air. I had no idea of the journey that awaited me, of the shadows I had to fearlessly explore, and of the healing that would welcome me home to myself.

The day I decided to leave my husband I saw the end of the rope as it was yanked from my hand. I had always heard the expression 'that was the end of the rope.' Then I actually saw it, and I knew it was time. I was matter-of-fact when I told him. I had no tears left to cry. A vastness of unknown territory lay beyond the rope but I strode confidently into it, strengthened by the conviction that this was a choice between death and life, between 'We' and 'Me.' I chose life. I chose 'Me.'

Over the last four years I have told and retold the story of the journey to me. As I have healed, and forgiven myself and my ex-husband, my perspective has changed and the way I tell my story has changed. This is to say that the story of your life is elastic. How you tell your story makes all the difference in how you view your life. When I started telling my story, it was about what he did to me and how I was a victim in my marriage. As I healed myself, my story shifted. I now choose to own the power to write my story, and to navigate the course of my life. I choose to tell a story of self-discovery and empowerment.

What do you choose?

Exercise

Obtain a deck of Tarot cards and spread them out face-down. With clear intention, choose a card to represent your past, a card to represent your present situation, and a card to represent your future. Looking at the images on the cards, write the story of your divorce. Begin with "Once there was a prince/princess who had to make a difficult decision..." Write a paragraph for each card which represents the past, present and future of your mythic story. Read your story aloud to a close friend, and see how you feel as you hear yourself tell your story from this new mythic perspective. Feedback is welcome from your friend, limited to "I heard your voice falter at this part" or "I really believed this part of the story." Our subconscious works in mysterious ways through the power of telling a story; learn what's going on under the surface in your own mind by giving this a whirl.

Not quite done yet

Right before the fires of destruction exploded, I experienced this period of limbo I like to call 'not quite done yet.' During this time period I found myself wanting to go back to sleep, making excuses, and drinking heavily. It was an emotional oscillation that I wanted to ignore because looking at it meant I had to do something about it, and doing something about it meant big changes I wasn't prepared to make. It was a period of extreme indecision and confusion, and it lasted longer than the other times that I couldn't decide whether I loved him, hated him, or didn't care anymore. If you go through this, you may find yourself reluctant to give in to "I'm sorry," and yet you really want to believe "I'm sorry" more than ever. You may find yourself expanding the boundaries of what you previously thought you could tolerate for the sake of 'making it work,' and trying to convince yourself that maybe you just didn't know your own mind and crossing all these lines is making it better. You may find yourself not knowing yourself any longer. This is a precarious place where the 'right' answer is hard to come by...until the moment you know it through and through.

Falling asleep in the Poppy Field

The worst place you can be in your long term relationship is asleep in the Poppy Field. I used to believe that was the best place in the world because it felt 'safe' and 'comfortable' and I could 'rely' on it. Now I see that the safety and comfort created in the Poppy Field are delusions based on assumptions that the person I am romantically involved with shares the same perspective of the world as me and 'knows me' better than I know myself, and that nothing in our relationship will ever change so I can relax and fall asleep. The closest association I can make to what happens when you wake up from sleeping in the Poppy Field is this: What

11

happens after a night of downing Tequila shots? The hangover from waking up after a dozen years of marriage and two kids to find that you and your spouse share very little in common with your underlying belief structures is also called a rude awakening.

Basing a relationship on assumptions leads to a very difficult negotiation at the best, and a heart-wrenching divide to your family at the worst. That warm dreamy feeling you have at the beginning of a relationship is where you start falling asleep to the narcotic invitation of those seductive Poppies and is the exact time you need to stop and get things very, very clear. Questions are your best friend at the start of a relationship and a great way to sober up. Questions remain your ally in a relationship because the truth is, people *change* over time and therefore the agreements holding a relationship together also change.

If you are now in the middle of your hangover from falling asleep in those darned Poppies, hug yourself and get on with the lessons you need to learn to get through *this moment*. I recommend picking up a copy of *The Four Agreements* by don Miguel Ruiz, and turning to the section about Not Making Assumptions. Here's an apropos quote:

> *Don't make assumptions. By making this one agreement a habit, your whole life will be completely transformed. If you don't make assumptions, you can focus your attention on the truth, not on what you think is the truth. Then you see life the way it is, not the way you want to see it. –don Miguel Ruiz*

Some assumptions are so sneaky they appear to be truth and in a conscious relationship we can agree to keep each other awake by asking lots of questions to uncover the truth that is begging to be revealed. Clear communication is vital to a healthy relationship, but often in an unconscious relationship we can make assumptions that our partner 'knows' what we want. These assumptions lead to hurt feelings whenever our expectations are not met.

Making assumptions in relationships leads to a lot of fights, a lot of difficulties, a lot of misunderstandings with people we supposedly love. Often we make the assumption that our partners know what we think and that we don't have to say what we want. We assume they are going to do what we want because they know us so well. If they don't do what we assume they should do, we feel hurt and say, "How could you do that? You should have known." –don Miguel Ruiz

I spent my entire marriage asleep in the Poppy Field, expecting he would 'know' what I wanted when often the truth was...I didn't know myself what I wanted. From this I learned another truth: *You're the only person who can figure out what you want.*

The problem starts with
Til Death Do Us Part

Growing up in Western society you might have thought that there was one right way to do marriage: *til death do us part.* See if this sounds familiar: I will do everything I can to make you happy, I will never ever have sex with another person, I will change myself and deny my own needs if that is what is needed to make this marriage work. See which of the following statements you have adopted:

- If I don't like something you're doing, you need to change it.
- If I want you to do something to make me happy, you have to do it.
- If you have sex with another person, you deserve to be punished.
- You can't make a (big/small) decision in your life without consulting me first.

Review the arguments in your marriage. Chances are they occurred when one of these basic tenets was violated. The problem with societal constructs is that they assume one size fits all. The marriage construct is so pervasive in our consciousness (talk shows, movies, family discussions, and church sermons) that we might think that is the ONLY way to be in sacred partnership, and we might never ask this question: *What is true for ME?*

Without exploring the questions *What is true for ME?* and *What is true for YOU?,* you end up in a one-size-fits-all system of control and judgment that will inevitably create discord within your marriage because it's not *true* and it's disempowering for each person in the relationship.

The quicksand of self-doubt

It's possible to entirely lose yourself within the couple dynamics so that you no longer know who you are outside of that relationship. Lots of little stories are told every day within that common reality called marriage and those stories become more and more real unless you are actively engaged in other long-term friendships that remind you of the 'you' that shows up in other relationships. The fear of change (along with guilt and shame) can create a great deal of self-doubt that keeps you mired in a situation that is not beneficial for your continued growth. Are those things your spouse says about you 'true'? Or are those things projections onto you of unconscious patterns/behaviors/beliefs your spouse doesn't want to admit about himself/herself? How about the other way around? What things do you complain about regarding your spouse? Is it possible these things are actually your own shadow?

The more entwined you are with your spouse, the more difficult it becomes to answer any of these questions. If you have lost touch with who you are, and do not deeply and intimately have awareness of your own shadow and submerged belief structure, then how can you differentiate what is your 'stuff' versus your spouse's 'stuff'?

To add to the complication, many of our first intimate relationships mirror to us the dynamics under which we were raised in our families. The shadow side of these family dynamics present areas of growth for us, and are woven into the fabric of our intimate romantic relationships to give us the opportunity to 'work it out.'

14

These uncomfortable dynamics can make you question yourself as the love potion wears off and you start to realize your spouse is treating you exactly the same way you perceived your mother or father or siblings did when you were growing up.

Once children enter the picture, the shadow dynamics from your own childhood can change you, how you feel about life, and how you feel about your spouse. You might notice personality changes in your spouse with the additional responsibility of being a mother or father. The primal constant needs of children can wear down any person's resources, especially in cases where children are colicky or excessively demanding of attention. You can end up feeling depleted, questioning yourself as a parent, arguing with your spouse over the 'right' course of action, and wanting more time to yourself. Body issues can creep into the marriage due to less time to focus on self-care, and these issues can further disrupt self-worth and marital intimacy. Negative internal messages can be heightened during this time, and lead to more argument. It is difficult to conduct a marriage with your internal versions of your mother and father 'advising' you, your actual mother and father 'advising' you, your spouse's internal and external versions of mom and dad 'advising' you, friends 'advising' you, the media 'advising' you, and so on. All of these voices create internal pressure and noise that can become unbearable when not dealt with in a conscious, aware manner.

In my marriage, the noise generated fear about doing things the 'wrong way' and this spawned the 'right' and 'wrong' game; the sole intent of this game was to control the voices and validate couple choices in the marriage and in parenting. A way of life and belief system evolved that mandated 100% agreement between us, and so the person with the loudest argument, greatest body of proof, or determination in being 'right' was able to set the family 'rule.' Whatever person had to succumb to the new 'rule' would feel a measure of disempowerment and self-doubt as a result. And since the 'right way' was largely influenced by unconscious ancestral patterns that were very strong and validated from familial mirrors (our parents) and friends (who we chose because they think like us), the resistance to letting go of the personal 'right way' in favor of the marital agreement was strong because it was like releasing self-identity and questioning the inherent intelligence of one's family lineage. We retreated to couples therapy because we needed a referee in these debates, and actually had to create a code word to use to stop the arguments. I was in it until death, however, and I was determined to do my part. I knew that marriages were 'work' and I was committed to doing what it took.

As it happens, while my husband and I were playing the 'one right answer' game, I was simultaneously being exposed to people doing things different ways with success, and noticed how there seemed to be more than one right answer for every situation. The idea that there was more than one 'right' answer did not fit into the 'right' and 'wrong' game of our marriage, and so whenever I would point out different approaches I learned from friends, this would fuel a new debate.

The moment I realized that not everyone was experiencing the same kind of marriage as me, and that not everyone had the same marital and parenting rules, a crack in the foundation of our marriage began. This crack deepened with each debate. And at some point, it dawned on me that we were creating this situation for ourselves through our unspoken beliefs. When I realized that my beliefs were creating my reality, I also realized I could change my beliefs and change my experience of life. It took me several years to truly own this realization, but once it sank deep enough I was able to cut through the self-doubt and take action leave the relationship and work on myself. Whether you invest in your relationship or leave it, there is no escaping working on yourself if you want freedom in your life and in your relationships.

Confusion and anger are normal
in the asylum

Living with your sacred mirror, that person who reflects to you all that you are, faced every moment with that most accurate portrayal of your glories and imperfections, creates deep vulnerability. It is wonderful and terrifying and gut-wrenching and beautiful. This is how the mirror works: it shows us where we like ourselves (those things you really like about your spouse that you actually like about yourself) and also where we are hurting (those things your spouse says or does that trigger you because deep inside there is a wound being touched). When we are unconscious, seeing the mirror of the things we don't like about ourselves can cause us to be angry and resentful; without a conscious attempt to work on these issues, couples can go crazy with the unhealed reflections they see in each other. The more personal work you do, the more you embrace yourself, the easier it is to stand in front of your mirror and accept what you witness.

I spent a lot of time in denial during my marriage so I really hated looking in my mirror at my shadows and faults. I preferred to intoxicate myself on wine and distract myself by spending money so I could be drunk on Poppies, and then blame my spouse for all the ways I abused myself whenever my shadow appeared. I preferred to believe someone 'out there' would love me better, would 'know me' and 'make me happy.' My spouse's criticisms cut deeply because it was all the same judgments I had for myself. I hated him for telling me what I already knew: I wasn't good enough, I was worthless, and I was broken. If I had healed my deep wounds, I would have been neutral or curious with my spouse's criticisms. As it was, I was devastated and it eventually became so painful that I left the marriage.

I believe it's possible that some relationships are designed to tear us down so we will face our shadows, and other relationships are rewards for having faced the mirror and accepted ourselves. If you haven't dived deep into your worst fears about yourself, and healed those wounds festering in your cracked childhood foundation, then how can you expect your spouse to mirror anything other than your self-loathing?

Of course you're confused and angry after facing your mirror. Until you've healed those deep wounds, you're living in the asylum baby.

The breakdown of intimacy

Complete honesty is an essential ingredient for intimacy, and often is lacking in a long-term relationship. Honesty ends up taking a backseat to roles and expectations and compromises. Without honesty, our emotional intimacy can shut down because we are blocking our own truth out of fear of creating conflict. When emotional intimacy shuts down, the love channel is constricted out of fear of rejection. Fear is the opposite of love. When fear enters the relationship dynamics, it brings jealousy and control. Jealousy and control kick out freedom to 'lock up' love, but freedom and love are a pair that travel together.

Without freedom and love, emotional intimacy diminishes, and as a consequence, sexual intimacy also fades away. How many times did you settle for unsatisfactory sex because you couldn't figure out a more exciting way to do it this time or because you were simply too tired to care? It's pretty hard telling your spouse "I'm bored with having sex with you." Have you ever done that? Even just imagining having that conversation, and then feeling the repercussions of days of resentment (and internal guilt) that would surely result were enough to deter me from this level of honesty.

What I noticed in my marriage was how we would be in a stream of sexual alignment for a while, and then would go out of alignment. Whenever I felt the lack of alignment was when I really didn't want to have sex with him, but then would acquiesce because I didn't want to deny him sex and be labeled in any of the familiar derogatory ways. Abandoning myself in this way caused more harm that it was worth in the long term. I stuffed the resentment which led to an underlying level of anger at myself for choosing to do something I did not feel like doing at the time.

I realize that people enter the marital relationship having had different levels of sexual experience. In my case, I had minimal sexual experience and my husband had even less than me. In our culture, sex is taboo to talk about, and this can lead to circumstances like the fact that I did not actually experience a true clitoral orgasm until I was 38 years old! What?? I was too embarrassed and uncomfortable with my sexuality to explore sex toys, vibrators and different partners. Therefore, much of my marriage was spent in a novice territory of sex that felt good, but that did not result in orgasm. Once I had my first undeniable orgasm, I simultaneously had two reactions: delighted and wanting to explore all the ways to have more orgasms; and deep resentment that my husband had experienced this incredible sensation for 16 years and I didn't (*and he knew that I was missing out!*). It was a couple of years into my healing spiritual journey before I could take personal responsibility for the fact that I had not explored my own sexual pleasure until later in life.

No matter what your level of sexual experience is when you enter a marital arrangement, it is difficult to 1) have sex with the same person for a prolonged period of time, 2) accept never having sex with anyone else, 3) deal with the fact that you are sexually attracted to different people you meet who are not your partner, and 4) respond to control and jealousy from your partner. Once you realize that different people provide uniquely fulfilling sexual encounters, curiosity is a compelling enemy to monogamy. For example, if you ate oatmeal for sixteen years every single morning because that was the only breakfast available, and then one day you had French toast…don't you think that would be the most delicious French toast you could ever imagine? (Especially if you knew you wouldn't be forced to eat French toast every day for the next sixteen years?)

What underlies a cheating heart

During my marriage, I had extramarital sexual experiences more times than I can remember, or want to remember. Each time I would have one of these encounters—always on the road at an art show—I would come back home and admit my infidelity to my husband. Now that I understand myself better, and have the perspective of time, I see how this behavior was not only because I was finally experiencing my sexuality, but it was a rebellion from the deep criticism I felt in my marriage and in myself. It was a rebellion that only served to prove the point that I was worthless, to myself and to him, because I knew that 'cheating' was 'wrong.' Continuing to have these one-night stands was like saying, "You think I am not good enough? You think I am flawed? Let me show you how bad I really am."

It's true that my ex-husband was, and is, a very critical person. But deeper than that, more cutting and damaging than that, was my own self-judgment. With his critical remarks, he was only mirroring to me my own self-loathing, my own certainty that I would never be good enough.

Anger was underneath the surface of my cheating, fueling it. I was furious to be judged and critiqued and controlled. "I'll show you" was certainly a thought that went through my head thousands of times, if I had been paying attention to my thoughts at that time. When another man noticed me, desired me, and wanted me, it was like proof that my ex-husband (and my inner voice) was wrong. "This man sees my value! How come he sees it but you can't?" I would also concoct fantasies that with a different man, I would be appreciated and treated *right*. I was sure that my ex-husband and his critical ways were the complete source of my unhappiness in life; if he would only learn to be supportive, I could be happy. Or if I could just find the *right* man who *appreciates* me, I would be happy.

The momentary victory I felt when a man was attracted to me and paid me attention would quickly vanish as the mirage faded and the truth was revealed time and again: I was simply a means to quick pleasure for the men who came with me to my hotel rooms. At the time I tangled up sex with self-worth, so it got very messy in my mind and heart. My inner judge ate this up like candy and made me pay for my transgressions with even more censure. Any tiny bit of self-worth I had derived from the attention and praise from these men was quickly shattered: "All they want is to have sex with you. They don't care about you." This was only exacerbated when my husband was unfazed by the cheating; and I felt even more debased when he wanted to take it to the next level and do couples swinging. With the perspective of time, I can see how swinging was an obvious suggestion for my ex-husband to make; this solution would offer transparent sexual experimentation for us both. However, when your self-worth is tied up in your sexuality, and you've set yourself up to feel shame and censure with your sexuality because you're operating from the monogamy 'rule book,' and your sexcapades are really more about rebellion, what do you think the end result of your self-worth is? It's a downward spiral of self-loathing leading to blaming the spouse leading to rebellion leading to acting out leading to critique and self-judgment leading to more self-loathing. The spiral goes down until you hit rock bottom and there's nowhere lower to go. I was not in a place of being comfortable with how I was coloring outside the lines sexually, and I wasn't in a mature space spiritually from which to take personal responsibility for my own truth. Therefore, with the spotlight on my uncomfortable sexual explorations, the marriage became so painful that I ended it.

> *You have a limit to the amount of abuse you will accept, but no one in the world abuses you more than you abuse yourself. The limit of your self-abuse is the limit you will tolerate from other people. If someone abuses you more than you abuse yourself, you walk away, you run, you escape. But if someone abuses you a little less than you abuse yourself, perhaps you stay longer. You still deserve that abuse.*
> *—don Miguel Ruiz*

Control through jealousy and ownership issues

If you are at the place in your marriage where your spouse monitors your cellphone, email, Facebook, and all other forms of communication, you might stop and consider why you are allowing another person to control you in this manner? Are you a teenager again, grounded in your room? Do you think you deserve to be constantly questioned, monitored, and assumed guilty of transgressions? Even if you have previously committed adulterous crimes, if your spouse agrees to continue in relationship with you, then that is his/her choice to accept you as you are, 'flaws' included.

In the track of fear we have so many conditions, expectations, and obligations that we create a lot of rules just to protect ourselves against emotional pain, when the truth is that there shouldn't be any rules. These rules affect the quality of the channels of communication between us, because when we are afraid, we lie. If you have the expectation that I have to be a certain way, then I feel the obligation to be that way. The truth is I am not what you want me to be. When I am honest and I am what I am, you are already hurt, you are mad. Then I lie to you, because I'm afraid of your judgment. I am afraid you are going to blame me, find me guilty, and punish me.
—don Miguel Ruiz

In my post-divorce philosophy, after recovering from co-dependency, I have come to the realization that nobody 'owns' anybody but themselves. I think the best solution to the jealousy issue is being honest with yourself about what you can actually agree to, and then clearly communicating that to your spouse, preferably at the start of the relationship (and anytime your internal agreement shifts). For example, if you cannot agree to monogamy, then do not agree with monogamy; allow your spouse the freedom to choose where his/her boundaries are with respect to your honest communication of the agreements you can abide by.

A relationship where control through jealousy is the norm is rooted in fear and disrespectful of the 'Me' in the 'We.' The flower of love cannot grow in a jealous relationship, and eventually will drop dead on the vine.

Extricating 'Me' from 'We'

My first glimpse of 'Me' was when the decision to leave my marriage turned like a key in a lock in my heart. The how and when were secondary to what and why, and resolved themselves with lightning quick synchronicities. Once the decision was made to leave my marriage, I had everything I needed the moment I needed it. Before I knew it, I was out of the 'We' and in new unknown territory of rediscovering the lost 'Me.' I had to extricate all that was 'We' so I could figure out what 'Me' actually was.

Sometimes you need to walk away from a relationship to see what's left. As the ocean liner pulls out, its wake causing ripples in your harbor, you can finally tell who YOU are because you're the only one left standing at the shore. Isn't that a blessing to finally know who you are? Trust that it's worth it to love yourself enough to stand alone.

Survival first

The first step after ending a significant relationship is to get the big rocks in the box: shelter, food, safety, and emotional support. In the weeks before I shared the news of my impending departure with my husband, I reviewed my finances, contacted my clients, and made a general game plan for how I was going to support myself. I assumed no help from him. Really, I just didn't want one more argument.

In hindsight, I wish I could have asked for support in the divorce settlement. At the end of my marriage, however I had very little self-esteem. With all the flagrant violations of my marriage I had demonstrated concretely how I was in the 'wrong.' More subtle and hidden in the shadows of our marriage were all the tiny daggers over the years that had eroded my self-worth to the point where I acted out in protest and became the outward manifestation of how worthless I felt. There was no fight left in my heart to make a major accounting of minor persistent slights; all that was left was flight.

Years later, I met professionals who are well versed in helping people to garner a fair split in a divorce; I would have loved this kind of help, if only I had felt worthy of it. I most definitely encourage anyone who is contemplating divorce to consult with a financial planner who can accurately assess a fair division of assets, and to hire a divorce coach or therapist as a guide through the process.

One gift I did give myself throughout my marriage was to keep up a professional career, even if it was only part-time. During my marriage I often felt jealous of friends whose husbands paid all the bills, while mine wanted me to work to earn money for the extras. When it was time to leave, I was thankful. By retaining my ability to generate revenue, I had enough power to be able to walk out of the marriage and support myself. Also, having clients allowed me to immerse in work and the act of providing for my household. I had less time to dwell on the emotional aspects of the divorce while occupying my mind with work projects.

With my decision to leave my marriage was a willingness to let go of everything not essential to my survival. The first wave of moving happened solo while my husband was at work, stuffing trash bags with clothing and shoving my most important items into the minivan. I wanted to avoid a confrontation at all costs since I was not sure how he would react. In the end, our separation was a somber but respectful process, and so there had not been a need on my part to worry. By acting as I did, however, I saved myself and my husband needless emotional upheaval. The rest of the moving process happened with my husband willingly away from the house while friends and family helped me move my belongings. Thus, the division of assets began.

A blessing of my separation from my husband was that there was very little greed and acrimony exhibited in the process. Both of us seemed to hold the intent to disengage from the marriage in as fair a way as possible. Acceptance of the inevitable is very helpful at this stage of separation. Realizing that this decision to separate marks the end of 'working on it,' it is nonetheless important to maintain civility in all interactions. Later on, with time and reflection, I thank myself for avoiding drama and hurtful words when we parted. While the transition of ending a long-term love relationship can be deeply painful, the relationship is worth the honor of courteous communication and behavior.

What helped me to keep interactions respectful when going through separation and divorce was to:

- Let go of being 'right' or convincing your former spouse of your point of view. Once you've decided to end the marriage, it can only create friction to persist in the negotiations or debates you used to have in the relationship.
- Avoid the kind of adversarial attitude that leads to fighting over assets. When we have the energy of attachment, it's easy for an angry ex to lash out by refusing to let go of whatever it is we think we want in the settlement. However, entering negotiations with a fair-minded, compassionate, tolerant disposition can help you more easily negotiate to retrieve the assets you believe you deserve.
- Inject business-like professionalism into your communications with your former spouse. Start perceiving your ex as you would a person at work with whom you have a challenging relationship, and do your best to communicate cleanly and clearly. Employ simple factual *neutral* statements.
- End emotional interactions and allow space and time for things to cool down before resuming negotiations. Perhaps if you were engaged in-person and the discussion became heated, wait a couple of days and send a well thought-out email (remembering that everything communicated via email becomes a chain of evidence for divorce proceedings). Absolutely avoid all contact while under the influence of drugs or alcohol.
- Claim responsibility for your part in the ending of the relationship.
- Find new sources of support for yourself. Continuing to reach out to your former spouse for advice or help is going to blur the lines of what is actually occurring—separation of two lives—and lead

to frustration. Make new friends, hire professional help, and start leaning on yourself for support.

- Nurture yourself with regular exercise, a healthy diet, massage, and meditation. During this stressful time, it is more important than ever to give your body, mind and spirit what you need to cope. Also remember that alcohol is a depressant, so although it can feel relaxing, it can also further plummet one's emotional state.

Using the Period

When a significant relationship ends, the inner judge goes into overdrive trying to figure out who was 'wrong' and what decisions/words/actions led to this predicament. A massive cover-your-ass effort ensues to review all interactions great and small for the entire duration of the marriage to prove that you were 'right' and not at fault for this extremely uncomfortable situation of losing everything you had worked so hard to gain. Whew! It's a lot of mental hoops that are incredibly unnecessary.

Every time your mind starts down the twisting corridors of 'right' and 'wrong' and 'he/she said' and 'your fault,' the best strategy is to put a Period on it. You have heard the story a million times already as it cycled on hyper-drive inside your skull. Do you really need to hear it again? Do you think you have the perspective necessary, in this moment, to understand what just happened?

Once I learned about the Period from HeatherAsh Amara, I discovered an all new appreciation for brevity of thought. When I experienced the freedom of "He said it's my fault my son is failing science PERIOD" rather than letting my attention get hooked with usual run-on sentence of guilt-ridden and angry thinking that could continue for hours, it created a satisfying gap into which I allowed silence. Reflect on the chaos in your brain at this moment. Can you do anything to influence the opinion of your soon-to-be-ex at this juncture in time? Does your ex's opinion really matter within the context of you starting out on your own journey of life? If you can answer no to both of those questions, then you see how relaxing it can be to put a Period on the thought and let go of the rest of the run-on sentence. Put a big pause on trying to figure out where to place blame; by the time you're done with this book, I'm hoping you'll understand that strategy is pointless.

Later on, when you are safe and have the energy to devote to introspection, you can let the rest of the sentence continue and observe it as a neutral witness.

Not taking it personally

Whatever your former spouse is saying or doing has nothing to do with you. You certainly *feel* the impact of your former spouse's actions and words, and your life is going to *change* as a direct result of these actions and words, but it still has nothing to do with **you**. It has everything to do with the perception of you that your spouse created from his/her own projections and filters. I'll talk about sacred mirrors later in the book, but for now the key thing to understand is not taking it personally. For example, let's assume your spouse is cheating on you and leaving you to run off with a new person. Your mind might be saying things like 'I'm not good enough,' 'I couldn't make her/him happy,' 'What's wrong with me?' Your spouse leaving you for another person has nothing to do with you. Even if your spouse says 'I prefer this other person because she/he is beautiful and you are not.' Still this has nothing to do with you. It has everything to do with your spouse's perceptions, belief system, priorities, and vision of life.

The key to understanding the second agreement of *Don't Take Anything Personally* (from *The Four Agreements* by Don Miguel Ruiz) is to become like an eagle and fly high in the sky. From this bigger perspective, you can see that there are millions of people, each living their own dream of life, each believing they are the center of the Universe. If you dropped to view a single person, you would see an entire web of beliefs wrapping that person up like a fly in a spider's web; this web is so much a part of the person that he/she doesn't even know it's there. It's like fish do not know they are swimming around in water; except maybe the fish that jumps into the air and get a different perspective by having a new experience. The entire way a person sees life, perceives events and interactions, and chooses how to respond is based on the quality and contents of the web that surrounds him/her.

Nothing other people do is because of you. It is because of themselves. All people live in their own dream, in their own mind; they are in a completely different world from the one we live in. When we take something personally, we make the assumption that they know what is in our world, and we try to impose our world on their world.
—don Miguel Ruiz

If someone says or does something to you that hurts you, you take it personally and believe these words or actions are about you. But the words or actions of this person are not about you—it's about *them*. Another person's words or actions can only ever be about them, about their dream of life, because the only thing a person understands is his/her own dream.

If someone gives you an opinion and says, "Hey, you look so fat," don't take it personally, because the truth is that this person is dealing with his or her own feelings, beliefs, and opinions. That person tried to send poison to you and if you take it personally, then you take that poison to you and it becomes yours. Taking things personally makes you easy prey for these predators, the black magicians. They can hook you easily with one little opinion and feed you whatever poison they want, and because you take it personally, you eat it up. —don Miguel Ruiz

If something that someone says or does to you hurts you, it is because you agree with it on some level; it is because it touches a wound that exists within you already. If you allow this pain to create suffering within you, you drink the poison and hurt yourself.

Humans are addicted to suffering at different levels and to different degrees, and we support each other in maintaining these addictions. Humans agree to help each other suffer. If you have the need to be abused, you will find it easy to be abused by others. Likewise, if you are with people who need to suffer, something in you makes you abuse them. It is as if they have a note on their back that says, "Please kick me." They are asking for justification for their suffering. Their addiction to suffering is nothing but an agreement that is reinforced every day. —don Miguel Ruiz

The invitation is to flip your perspective around interactions with others that cause you suffering. Instead of being concerned with why the other person did or said x or y, become interested and curious about why *you* feel a reaction to it. Clean up the agreements and beliefs within yourself that allowed you to experience pain because of an interaction, and even choose different people with whom to interact so that you build the kind of life you want to live every day.

If someone is not treating you with love and respect, it is a gift if they walk away from you. If that person doesn't walk away, you will surely endure many years of suffering with him or her. Walking away may hurt for a while, but your heart will eventually heal. Then you can choose what you really want. You will find that you don't need to trust others as much as you need to trust yourself to make the right choices. —don Miguel Ruiz

Getting your sea legs

When you've spent any length of time in the predictable monogamous relationship space, and then you're suddenly out at sea in the choppy water of uncertainty, you can feel pretty wobbly trying to get your balance with all the changes happening in rapid fire. It can leave you feeling like there is no safe place to step that isn't going to drop out from underneath you.

If you are the kind of person that thrives on having the 'right' answers, it might feel very overwhelming to suddenly be thrust into a world you do not understand. This is a perfect time to adopt "Don't know" mind and become curious to learn about this new world, much like a scientist conducts experiments without determining the outcome in advance. Enjoy the liberation of answering questions about your future with 'I don't know.' One day you might enjoy the mystery of *not* knowing.

Avoiding blaming your ex

The problem with blame is that it is the *opposite* of standing in your power. When we want to blame someone for our life situation, what we are really doing is standing on the Triangle of Disempowerment at the Victim corner. The only possibility in the Victim corner is to suffer because you have no power to change your circumstance: you cannot control the Perpetrator who has power over you, and you don't know when the Rescuer is going to arrive. The moment you step off the Triangle of Disempowerment and claim personal responsibility, everything changes because **you decide** it is going to change.

"But my spouse did X and now that is affecting me negatively." Yep. Probably there is a deeper truth about the role you played in the situation as well. For example, did you stay in the situation *knowing* that X was happening and that it was negatively affecting you? The point here is that perception through a dirty lens is not clear and factual, it's distorted. There are often several ways to view situations at the end of the marriage, and each party can justify their point of view according to their own dirty lens. No matter who is 'at fault,' cleaning up the mess from your side of the fence is taking personal responsibility and empowering yourself. Lingering in the blame game keeps you engaged in a disempowered way in the relationship. Stepping into personal responsibility and making active decisions to resolve outstanding issues and move forward in your life will *liberate* you.

Losing your couple friends

One of the hardest hitting aspects of divorce happens at the same time as your divorce: losing the friendships you thought were for *you*, and realizing that those friends were only part of the phase of your life when you belonged to a *couple*. Part of the reason these friendships often fall apart is that, by their very nature, they no longer fit your life. You are not part of a couple anymore, and those friendships were designed to support and extend your marriage.

Once you become a single person, you can be seen or felt as a threat to the stability of your couple friends' relationships. Perhaps divorce is like a disease that can be caught? Or with your newfound liberation from the marriage contract, you experience a sexual liberation that your couple friends find threatening? Certainly, divorce is a heavy topic that people going through it want to talk about incessantly, and this is difficult for those people *not* going through it. Each situation is unique, but it does seem that these themes are prevalent.

If you happen to have made couple friends who want to maintain connection with you, honor those friendships by not putting them in the middle of your divorce. Couple friends who liked both you and your spouse will likely feel uncomfortable listening to your side of the story because it makes them feel like they have to choose sides. When the marriage first ends, we don't have a great deal of perspective to see that there are multiple sides to this divorce story; but there are, and your couple friends can witness this fact.

Find new friends who do not know your former spouse so that you have the support you need as you mend from the divorce and grow into this new phase of your life.

Co-managing the kids

Years after our divorce my ex-husband and I went to counseling to develop a cohesive strategy for helping our son who was facing teen troubles. After a handful of sessions, our counselor looked at us and remarked "I don't know how the two of you ever got married. You're that different when it comes to personality, outlook, and parenting strategies." Oh, so that's why it was always so hard!

In my case what made it more difficult to co-parent with my ex-husband was how my own parents' opinions would inevitably coincide with my ex-husband's. I was usually alone in my parenting perspectives, which was, I realized, part of my spiritual lesson in this life.

So what I eventually decided to do was set some clear boundaries:

- Do not involve your parents or in-laws in parenting discussions. This means that you cannot grouse about your ex's parenting decisions. If you complain to your in-laws or your parents about the ex's parenting decisions, you invite them to share their perspective with you. If your ex is a dead ringer for your mother with whom you've fought your whole life, or is a twin to the father you don't get along with, you're just inviting trouble by involving them in your co-parenting glitches. The little bit of sympathy you receive will not be worth the mountain of disapproval for your parenting style.

- If in-person parenting discussions with your former spouse lead to a high level of frustration, consider conducting negotiations over email. If you choose this strategy, adopt a legal mind and professional business communication style to emails. Remember that every email is part of a chain of evidence should things go south. Do not fire off emails when angry. Using the email approach demands composure and patience.

- Set up a Google calendar to coordinate and share kids' activities among all parties who manage the children. A shared calendar makes it very easy to avoid misunderstandings or last-minute disruptions to plans or the 'I didn't know I was supposed to pick them up' excuse.

- Be as clear as possible about all facets of a decision and its ramifications. Consider all the impacts up front with clear thinking whenever making decisions about a course of action with the children.

- Do not complain to your children about your former spouse, and do not invite information about how things are going at your ex's house from your children. Comparison between the households is inevitable; however, you can minimize the negative effects by acknowledging the differences in approaches up front with your kids and reinforcing the rules of *your* house. Trust your own parenting instincts to create a structure at your house that feels *right for you*.

- Do not compare your children to yourself or your former spouse. They may share personality traits in common with one or both of you, but your child is his/her own person. Aligning your child with a parent based on personality traits creates division within a family that is insidious and painful and can lead to unconscious and unintended poor treatment of the child (in the place of the untouchable former spouse).

- Love is more important than any issue on the table when it comes to the kids. Hug your child for as long as they'll stay in your arms and tell them you love them more times in a day than you have breath to utter the words. Love heals the wounds of divorce, and assures the children they are safe and cared for even if the home doesn't include all the same people and things it used to.

Handling finances as a single parent

When I was part of a married couple, my husband held down the steady job while I provided the variable income with my consulting business. After we had children, I decided I wanted to pursue my artwork full-time. The resulting diminished consulting revenue caused a great deal of friction in our financial picture, and led to my husband's resentment of my art career. This wound continued to fester and was responsible for a large part of the acrimony in our marriage. My husband was focused on accruing material wealth, while I was more interested in fulfillment from creating artwork. It was here that our life streams diverged and never merged again.

The day I moved out of our family home I cried...when I left my art studio for the last time. It was the only aspect of the divorce that brought me to tears (and still does). We had built my art studio to my specifications to ensure the perfect daylight for working in color; it was beautiful with a two-story high ceiling, windows all along the north-facing wall, and huge doors to the south for moving large canvases in and out. It was my vision; my husband had agreed to it for the resale value as an in-law unit. At several points I considered staying in the marriage so I could keep the art studio. Eventually, staying married was more painful than leaving my beloved studio.

Once I was on my own, I found myself immersed in responsibility for all the finances necessary to support my household. Because I wanted to avoid any more arguing, I did not ask for child support or alimony in the divorce; we shared the kids 50/50 and so I was grateful for the time I had to myself. This meant, however, I had to support my household entirely by myself. I wanted to provide a comparable standard of living for my children even though I clearly had to downsize. I wanted each child to still have his own bedroom, and live in a nice area in a single home environment. These requirements could not be satisfied by an artist's income. The dream of working as an artist full-time was replaced with the reality of needing to generate revenue through consulting, a much more lucrative business than art. I had returned to consulting several years before the end of the marriage to placate my husband (and to pay for the studio construction), so I was equipped with enough revenue to support myself.

The irony is how I fought so hard to be an artist during the marriage, and then after the divorce there simply was not enough revenue from the artwork to allow me to support myself. Years later, what struck me was how amazingly lucky I was to have had my own custom-designed art studio; at the time, the shadows created by all the arguing over the art career prevented me from seeing how spoiled I was to have such decadence.

Following the divorce, I pursued a lot of personal development workshops, decided to go back to school and learn energy medicine, and spent a great deal on wellness and healing from the divorce and the painful effects of years of an unhappy marriage on my body, mind and spirit. All of these necessary life-rebuilding activities cost money, and created debt that, at the time, I just had to ignore and persevere in my transformation. Again, I was fortunate that the consulting jobs afforded me the extra revenue and security to pursue all these healing activities, even though I used credit to pay for a chunk of it in the whirlwind of completing my education while maintaining my household and managing the kids' schedules. Three years after the divorce the dust had settled sufficiently so that I could turn my attention towards getting my finances solvent.

Meeting with a financial advisor on a weekly basis, I started coming into alignment and right-relationship with my money. A good part of that process was taking a hard look in the mirror. At the first visit to my financial advisor I burst into tears. At the second meeting I cried again. I wondered if I would cry at every visit. Mind you, I had graduated from a very prestigious college and energy medicine school at this point, was an inspirational coach and speaker, and helped lots of people overcome fear and anxiety and feelings of worthlessness. I was a smart gal, spiritually sound, and I was bawling like a baby in front of my financial advisor.

During my marriage, I had been that woman who wanted champagne with brunch on a Sunday at a nice restaurant, manicured acrylic nails, and all-day spa visits for pampering. Since the divorce I prepared pancakes at home for the kids, switched to short nails, and traded massages for energy healing with local masseuses. Now I was taking it one step further and deciding to cut out everything non-essential for the sake of paying off my debts. For the first time in my life, I was claiming responsibility for my financial mess and making a hard effort to clean it up all by myself—no one to rescue me.

For years I entertained fantasies about being rescued by Mr. Right; these fantasies only delayed me taking proactive actions to rectify my situation. I was positive that the 'right man' would swoop me up as soon as I was divorced and whisk me off to a tropical vacation. I had a lot of ideas about what would happen when I was single again. Three years into being single, and a lot of personal development work under my belt, I finally knew that being rescued by a man was the last way I wanted to start a new relationship. Being rescued would put me right back into the same situation from which I fled.

No. I wanted to rescue myself, come into right relationship with my money, and meet a new man as the best version of me I could offer. I was finally ready to tighten the belt because I loved myself and my freedom more than I needed to satisfy my ego.

Facing money issues is one of the biggest spiritual and personal challenges a person can overcome. It's one of the most pervasive ways we can feel like a victim in our lives. And it is a ripe cornucopia of shadows into which to shine the light of your awareness.

Breaking free energetically

When we are entwined with another person in a long-term relationship or marriage, our energy bodies grow together like the roots of two trees planted next to each other. Breaking free from the relationship requires detangling at multiple levels: mental, emotional, and energetic. Getting over the relationship on the mental and emotional levels may prove to be difficult until the energetic bonds or 'cords' are removed. Often when there are energetic cords between two people it is because we are dependent upon the other person, almost like a life-raft. Typically cords between people are formed for security reasons; it makes sense that there would be cords between husband and wife in a marriage where there is a degree of co-dependence.

An energetic cord to a person is the equivalent of a wire-tap to a phone; the cord allows us to 'feel' that other person at all times, and even receive energy from that person. If you are the one supplying the energy to the person at the other end of the cord, you might feel drained while in relationship with that person, and not understand why you are always tired. 'Feeding' another person with your energy eventually leads to a survival issue—it comes down to you or them.

If you are the one receiving energy through the cord from the other person, you might feel very threatened by the end of the relationship because it now becomes a survival issue for you. Where will your source of energy and support come from now that the other person is gone?

You can determine if you have energetic cords to your ex-spouse by dropping into your body awareness with a quiet mind, and then posing the question: 'Where in my body do I feel connected to my ex?' You will likely just 'know' that a connection exists at a certain area of your body. Often this connection will be in a chakra:

- The root chakra is near the genitals and is responsible for our feelings of security and connectedness. It is the chakra of self-preservation, personal survival and our identification with the physical world.
- The sacral chakra is near the womb, and is responsible for relationships, creativity, sexuality, control and money.
- The solar plexus chakra is the will center located in the center of your diaphragm, and it controls your determination and focus and personal power.
- The heart chakra is responsible for our love, compassion, and connection to our soul and to Spirit.
- The throat chakra is located at the base of the neck and controls our ability to speak our truth.
- The third eye is in the center of the forehead and controls our vision of our life, our clarity, and our intuition.
- The crown chakra is at the top of the skull and enables our connection to Spirit.

If your body scan and intuition tells you there are cords between you and your former spouse, it is advised that you seek help to have these cords removed. It is possible to cultivate enough self-awareness through practice and personal ritual to remove cords yourself. For the sake of this publication, I will simply say that they can be removed by a Reiki practitioner or a shamanic healer who understands how to remove cords. Below is an excerpt from *Awakening To Me* where I describe my first session with a Reiki practitioner to remove cords between myself and my ex-husband.

> *I learn from Kat, my Reiki energy healer, that to move forward in my life I need to sever my connection with my ex-husband energetically, and reclaim that energy for my own healing; it's a process called Cutting the Cords. During our session, she massages*

me until I am relaxed and ready for this energetic release, and then we do the visualization.

She tells me to visualize my ex-husband out there in the world, and then to visualize long braided cords of different colors extending from my body to his along my chakras, or energy points in my body. Seven chakras from the top of my head to my sit-bone: seven cords that bind. One by one, I visualize a giant pair of scissors cutting the cord that binds me to him from each chakra, releasing him and retracting my energy back into myself, and as I cut the cords I forcefully HUFF all the air out of my diaphragm. As I release him, I feel gratitude for all that we shared in our life together and peaceful acceptance for where we are today.

The method that I learned for removing energetic cords from the Four Winds Light Body School is very different than the Reiki method I used with Kat; however, both methods work. There are probably other methods of which I am unaware. Do your research and experiment to see what works for you. You will know when you have removed the cords because you will no longer feel compelled to think about your former spouse.

Beyond removing energetic cords, you can practice rituals like the relationship burial described in **Letting go of the past** to help yourself detach energetically and emotionally from the entanglement. It can also be helpful to review old photographs and memorabilia and do a ceremony to release the energy held in these items and bless them. Burning sage and 'smudging' these items can remove latent energy charge and cleanse them of negative energy, or energy from the relationship that is causing a negative reaction inside of you. Repeating a prayer like the Ho'Oponopono prayer while smudging the items can help you emotionally release and come to terms with the ending of the relationship: *I'm sorry. Please forgive me. I love you. Thank you.* Here is an excerpt from *Awakening To Me* where I describe smudging my wedding dress to let go of my marriage.

As I am cleaning my closet, I discover a large white garment bag at the back of the closet and I pull it out. My wedding dress. I unzip the bag and pull out the dress. It is still as beautiful as it was the day I wore it. I am filled with sadness. It is time to apologize to this dress, to the young woman who wore it all those years ago, and to forgive myself for ending my marriage so that my soul had space to grow.

I fill my seashell with white sage and light it. White smoke fills my room as I move about, lifting the smoke into recesses in my closet. I shake my rattle to break up negative energy and dislodge it from my belongings, from my space, from my wedding dress.

I repeat this mantra:

I'm sorry. Please forgive me. I love you. Thank you.

Images from my wedding ceremony, feelings from my youth, memories from my marriage, all swirl around inside me as I perform this cleansing ritual and release the sadness welling up inside of me. Regret and anger pass through me and out as I continue to chant:

I'm sorry. Please forgive me. I love you. Thank you.

I see the young woman I was the day I became a wife, filled with promise and hope and joy and love. Believing the honey of life would be tasted.

I'm sorry. Please forgive me. I love you. Thank you.

I see the young mother, overwhelmed with the stresses of caring for an infant, feeling incapable of comforting the wailing baby, not knowing what to do, not feeling like a good mother at all.

I'm sorry. Please forgive me. I love you. Thank you.

I see a woman running from herself, from her fears, from her truth. I see a woman staying so busy she has no time to consider that this life she has built is tearing her apart from the inside.

I'm sorry. Please forgive me. I love you. Thank you.

I see a woman finally choosing herself, choosing time and space to heal, choosing quiet and contemplation, choosing to leave behind all she has built as the dream of her life to start on a journey to a destination unknown.

I'm sorry. Please forgive me. I love you. Thank you.

Exhausted after what feels like hours, I lay my empty body across my bed and sleep peacefully.

Cleansing the body of emotional energy

A rocky marriage, and most certainly the divorce process, can generate a lot of toxic emotional energy—sadness, anger, fear, jealousy, depression, and so forth. Toxic emotional energy, when repressed or not adequately released from the body, can lead to dis-ease at all levels: mental, emotional, physical, and spiritual. This is because toxic emotional energy is heavier than normal emotional energy, and thereby causes a burden on our physical body. Have you ever been in a room where there was a huge argument? Did you feel the heaviness to the air that seemed to cling to you? Toxic emotional energy also emits a certain frequency that calls to it similar experiences where more of the same emotional energy can be generated.

In fact, when there is a lot of toxic emotion in the body caused from the fighting that can occur in a dissolving relationship, the emotion can be like the hot force of lava wanting you to erupt at any trigger. Releasing the latent emotional energy from your body will make it easier to resist engaging in the fighting.

There are several ways I have personally released toxic emotional energy from myself. I recommend all of them to remove the emotional energy from all levels of being:

- Energy healing. The energy healing I studied at the Four Winds Light Body School, and probably other forms as well, removes the affinity in the energy body for certain relationship engagements, as well as releases stuck emotions from the chakra system.

- Acupuncture. What I've noticed that acupuncture does is to integrate the shifts made during an energy healing session, and rebalance the body and the flow of energy through it. There are different specialties with acupuncture. A practitioner who performs psychosocial acupuncture can be specially attuned to track emotional energy in the body and help it to release.
- Flower essences. The Bach flower essences, in my experience, are wonderful at helping emotional energy to be released at the cellular level—in other words, from each individual cell of the body. There are different 'remedies' and you can visit a practitioner to find out which ones your body needs; the practitioner will perform muscle testing to determine what your body requires.
- Massage. Touch is a powerful way to release emotional energy from muscle tissue where it can get lodged, as well as nourish your body, mind, and spirit. A masseuse who also practices some form of energy work, such as Reiki, is desirable.
- Exercise. When you exercise, you breathe in clear energy through the air, and release stagnant energy from your body through your breath. Exercise moves the energy and helps you release the toxic emotions from your system, especially anxiety, frustration, and anger.

Reclaiming your energy

Before I ever understood energy, there was an innate awareness that I was 'giving' my husband my energy; it was in the language I used to describe how I was feeling at the end of the marriage. "I'm tired of lifting him up" and "I can't fill his cup anymore." When I began my training with my spiritual mentors, I finally understood what had been happening. At the energetic level, we make agreements with our spouse that we can be largely unaware of; I had an agreement to help my husband feel better by taking on his negative energy and processing it for him, and by giving him my 'happy' and positive energy.

Twenty years of living this unconscious energetic agreement resulted in years of personal stress and depression, and culminated in a Texas grapefruit-sized cyst on my ovary. I noticed after a couple of years of cutting cords, reclaiming my energy, and setting energetic boundaries, that I was feeling a lot better. My depression and anxiety went away, I was able to stay positive and motivated for longer and longer stretches, and my former destructive behaviors dissolved. I also noticed that as I detached from my ex-husband, he became tighter and tighter physically and energetically under the weight of all his own stress and negativity that he did not know how to process. He shrank a couple of inches in size, lost a lot of weight, and started having health issues; essentially, he collapsed inwards under the pressure. I put him on my altar and prayed for him from afar.

Recapitulation, an ancient Toltec practice, is a powerful way to reclaim your energy from the places you lost it: arguments, denying your truth, giving your energy away, taking on roles that are not authentic, forcing yourself to do things because of the couples-construct. It is a practice of meditation whereby you review your life history for places you lost personal power, breathe back into yourself your sparkly clean energy from the past, and breathe out any energy you took on that does not belong to you (returning it to the Earth). It helps you to reclaim your energy that got stuck in the past with your 'mistakes' and regrets, release judgements of yourself and others, let go of any place you are in emotional/energetic bind with other people, forgive yourself and others, and come to closure.

You can also use recapitulation to rewrite the past by envisioning how you wish it had been. Our minds do not know the difference between the 'actual' past and our imagined past, and so it can be very healing to imagine situations resolving in a new way of your choosing. It is your opportunity to rewrite the outcome and correct those "If I had only said this" realizations.

The process of recapitulation is more than just remembering and allowing yourself to be overwhelmed by memories. By going fully into the experience and feelings, to completely release them through personal choice, you can finally take back the power lost in those moments. You

> *can also 're-script' the event — change the ending — and turn the trauma into an act of power.*
> — *Gerry Starnes, M.Ed., Spirit Paths: The Quest for Authenticity*

When getting started with recapitulation, it is helpful to be guided in the process by a teacher. You will need to learn how to create and hold an energetic container into which to return the energy. You will need to learn how to return the energy to yourself cleansed of any negativity or heaviness. You will need guidance on how to respectfully release energy you took on that does not belong to you. Lastly, you will need to learn how to direct this returned energy towards a new intent in your life. Practiced with these clear principles and intentions, recapitulation is a powerful way to create dynamic shift in your life and relationships.

Taking the time to understand what happened

Before moving on from a significant relationship, it's incredibly helpful to take the time to be introspective. Delve into your feelings and experiences and beliefs around that relationship and figure out the lessons. Take some spiritual or personal development courses to understand what just happened to you in the course of living as a couple. The lessons learned from this relationship review could very likely save you from repeating the patterns with a new person.

I realize that every person who gets a divorce has a different story about what caused the ending of the marriage. All I can do in this book is relate my own story, and the insights and lessons I have earned from having gone through the experience. Perhaps you may nod in agreement, or feel relief that you're not the only one.

As I reviewed the vastness of time and space shared with my ex-husband over two decades I realized the overall experience was...unquantifiable, immeasurable, defying categorization or labeling, confusing, heart exploding and heart breaking, beyond my grasp and right in my face...all at the same time. When I began to tell a story about why it didn't work, there was immediately evidence to the contrary. It felt like an impossible conundrum, the millions of moments between two people bonded in the intimacy of marriage and parenthood. Just when I thought I had released it all, that I had let it go to allow new possibilities in my life, there was another layer rising up for my attention, demanding me to crack open my heart wider with compassion and understanding.

I learned many valuable lessons from taking this time to ponder my marriage; lessons that progressed my overall healing journey. These insights helped me to know myself better so that I could transform my life into a greater vision. Understanding my marriage, and why it didn't work, wasn't a weekend project at retreat; it took years of serious dedicated contemplation, and the lessons are still unfolding.

Primarily, I realized that I had lived in an extremely co-dependent relationship for the first two decades of my adult life. In many ways, I convinced myself this relationship mimicked my parents' marriage because I desperately wanted the 'right man' and a secure marriage. After years of spiritual and personal development, and hearing others' stories, I witness that this is a trap many people fall into— trying to recreate what their parents had, or trying to do the opposite. In either case, the construct of the marriage is based on decisions and preferences of other people—namely, your parents—and not based on your own personal discovery of what makes you happy. When I fell into this trap, I fell hard.

The first month I was dating my ex-husband he paid off my credit card from college. He had money saved away, and he was anxious that I was wasting money paying interest on my debt. He paid it off, and then instructed me to cut up my credit card. I did it. I let him rescue me, and in so doing, I lost personal power. The loss of personal power was at first a small price to pay in exchange for the feeling of being protected and secure in what was essentially a support straightjacket. Over the course of my marriage there was a long litany of important decisions where I realized I had to either engage in endless debate with a man who believed there was exactly one right way to do everything (his way), or succumb to his point of view and

Lied, subterfuge

lose power. With time and maturity, I started resenting this loss of power and many times acted out rebelliously when decisions didn't go my way. But I wasn't successful in challenging the golden rule in our marriage which was that we had to agree about everything; there was no freedom to just 'agree to disagree.' When my Mom would witness this dynamic, she would forcefully 'encourage' me to fight back; to which I would respond "I have to pick my battles, Mom." Did I mention how much I loathed conflict, having very early childhood experiences of violent disagreements between my first step-father and my Mom? Did I mention that my parents were very overprotective compared with my peers' parents, and I had a hard time speaking my truth, especially to my Mom, because I so desperately wished to avoid a fight? During my marriage review, it did not escape my attention how similar my ex-husband and my Mom were; both of them have regularly experienced profound levels of anxiety and fear-based thinking which seems to generate the need to control decisions in relationships. *Jack's childhood*

The dynamic between my husband and I led to two versions of me: the inner and the outer. It also led to cultivation of manipulative behavior to assuage potential arguments and 'get my way' a little easier. To this end, I played the role of geisha. I kept myself looking pretty with acrylic nails and the latest fashions, I entertained at countless parties as hostess extraordinaire, I planned activities and trips to keep everyone distracted and happy, I wore ridiculously small bikinis to the pool that barely covered my breasts, I pranced around in frilly lacy outfits for his pleasure. I was skilled at being sexy; after all, that's how I captured him (and how I got what I wanted from him).

Everything that was truly me, and for the inner me, he questioned endlessly and resisted. I loved drawing and painting. I loved being out in nature capturing the experience on canvas. And I wanted that to be my career. He saw things differently. I had earning potential as a technical writer, and could bring in a far greater salary to keep up our expensive lifestyle. I came to him as a geisha. I couldn't then rewrite the story and have depth; he wasn't interested in depth.

Eventually the smallest argument could send anger shooting up inside of me. Why? Because my essential self was being denied, caged, diminished, criticized, and even mocked with all of the masks I wore—*the masks I made myself wear.*

Knowing this truth allowed me to understand that my journey in leaving my marriage had been about letting my essential self tell her story. It was about clearing my throat and giving her a voice. It was about standing my ground, and persevering in the argument until I was heard. It was about discovering my preferences and doing things that made me happy.

I found out that I prefer the simple things like natural nails, wearing no makeup, and putting on clothes because they're comfortable and they express who I am inside. I love walking in the woods and sitting with my feet in a gurgling creek. I love sunshine on my face. I love my body just the way it is with its curves and poochy belly. I love not being on the roller-coaster ride of endless pleasure-seeking. Most of all, my essential self loves finally being at the surface of my existence—seen, heard, and present.

The more you can understand the dynamics of your past relationship, the more you are willing to look into your own shadows instead of pointing the finger at your ex, the more you can take responsibility for how you failed *yourself*, the more you can witness and embrace your own authenticity and live by your truth: the greater chance you have of experiencing a vastly more fulfilling relationship next time.

Letting go of the past

It's essential to let go of the past, to release the 'We' relationship so that you can move forward with your life. But we cannot let go from anger, sadness, or frustration; we can only release from love and gratitude and acceptance.

When I was releasing my marriage, and later a significant relationship in my dating life, I devised a method of helping myself to energetically, emotionally, mentally, and physically let go. I call it the relationship burial.

1. See a balanced truth of your partner by making a list of facts in two columns: Positive Interactions and Negative Interactions. Do this task without judgment; this is an exercise in being honest with yourself about the quality of the relationship as it has progressed over time. Putting these facts in black and white can help you see the relationship with clarity if you are prone to inner fantasies and reveries of the past, or if you are prone to demonizing your ex-lovers.

2. Honor the beautiful and sacred feelings you carried with you from this relationship. Regardless of the 'facts' as you have scribed them, the truth is you loved this person. To detach, you need to move the energy out of your body. Print out pictures of your lover and then allow yourself to feel all the mixture of emotions that arise when you think of him/her; as these emotions arise, blow them into the paper photographs. By doing so, you transfer the emotion from your body into the photographs for safe-keeping, acknowledging these feelings as one might remember a loved one at an actual funeral. This act creates a physical manifestation of the emotions that can be released with a burial.

3. Prepare and conduct a burial for the relationship. You are burying a loved one, and although there is no 'body,' the burial process is just as real and sacred. Dig a hole in the earth, place your lover inside (the photographs that embody your emotions), and surround him/her with rose petals. And now it is time for the eulogy. This is where gratitude finally arises. If this person actually died, and you were at the funeral, what would you want to say? What could you be thankful for? As gratitude arises, blow into the rose-lined grave the intentions you hold for thankfulness. It is in this moment that Spirit speaks astonishing truths that often will be just what you needed to understand to let go.

When I performed this ritual to release my first post-divorce lover, Z, I got a profound message from Spirit. The message was that I was never meant to have a long-term relationship with him. He was a beautiful and tasty carrot that Spirit dangled in front of my nose so I would step onto the path of personal transformation that eventually led to being an inspirational writer, teacher, coach and energy healer. None of what I am today would have happened without first falling in love with Z, and desperately wanting to become the kind of person he could love in return.

4. Trust that Pachamama (Mother Earth) will heal these deep wounds, and plant seeds from which will grow new love. Working in the Earth is sacred and powerful magic. We sprang from the Earth, we are nourished every day by the Earth, and we will return to the Earth when our time is up. Pachamama mulches decay and transforms it into new life. There must be death before birth can occur. Trust that Pachamama will mulch the energy held in the burial for your lost love, and as she transforms that energy into new life, you will feel new love swelling inside of you. Someday, the seeds you planted in this burial will grow into a romantic relationship that matches your heart's frequency and feeds your soul.

Keeping a headstone to mark the grave allows you a place to visit to remember this dream, to release any remaining attachment or express any newfound gratitude as the weeks and months go by. The headstone also keeps you honest whenever you are tempted to reconnect with your former lover.

Where's the other half?

After surviving the physical aspects of leaving the marriage, and working out the mechanics of sustaining my own household, a new awareness began to dawn. I was alone. For the first time in my life: single. I realized I had never lived without another person to complete me. I had only ever been one half of a whole. I met my husband when I was 22 years old and moved in with him five months later. We had only been separated a few times for a week or two when he went out of town on business, a few days for different business trips, and a couple of girls' weekends here and there, until I started doing art shows in the last few years of our marriage.

My Mom and step-Dad had encouraged me from an early age not to get married until my late twenties. Well, I got married at 28 to a man I moved in with at 22. I don't think that's what they meant. I was driven by hormones and internalization of societal expectations to 'get the man' so I could build the 'perfect life.' I was star-struck by the big moment—the across-the-room soul connection that I shared with this man—and I let it outweigh every objection raised along the way. We had a lot of fun together with copious distractions, which allowed me to ignore the behaviors and arguments and constructs that eventually brought an end to the marriage; all we had to do was keep the amusement park running, and we were in business.

The real problem with my marriage was that I didn't know myself yet. Because I didn't know myself yet, I didn't know where boundaries should go to make a healthy long-term relationship, and I didn't know what personality traits and preferences would best complement me to bring the smoothest ride. But I was afraid to be alone. From the time I was 15, I always had a boyfriend. I was a serial dater. With my choice to move in with my husband at 22, I denied myself the opportunity to find out who I was before I became part of a couple.

The undercurrent of my belief systems around relationship, and one I have heard resonate through our society as I have experienced it, is a message that if you are not part of a couple, you are lacking a vital element to your personal security. For me, this deep domestication evoked a kind of panic on occasion when I would allow myself to think about it.

Very likely, part of my panic was triggered from early childhood where I learned first-hand the importance of having a 'good man' in your life. My natural father was caught making inappropriate sexual advances towards me when I was just one, and my first step-father was a violent drunk. When my Dad showed up on the scene (I was 5), he was like a knight in shining armor come to save the day; and my

Mom and I definitely felt rescued. There were lots of conscious and unconscious messages throughout my childhood and into my teen years about the importance of finding the right man.

So if I had no man of my own, where was my security, my rock? Could I really survive on my own? As the months went by, I proved capable of paying my bills by myself, and yet these voices of doubt continued in the recesses of my awareness, rippling deep-seated fear through me. What's going to happen to me now? Will I be an 'old maid'? Will the floor drop out from underneath my feet?

At first, being alone was a relief. I was able to freely lounge in a bubble bath every night, glass of wine in hand, without anyone waiting impatiently for me to finish and come to bed so he could sleep. I had spaciousness to relax and pamper myself, to sleep in late if I wanted, to eat pizza for dinner instead of cooking, and to indulge in chocolate cake (without hearing remarks about my weight). I could work on art in my garage studio without having to respond to phone calls and text messages if I did not want to; in fact, I pacified myself and changed settings to put my ex-husband on silent. I was able to make decisions without having to compromise with anyone, or endlessly debate why I wanted to do whatever it was I wanted to do. I was able to have peace and quiet without needing to talk when I didn't feel like talking. I was able to establish some boundaries for myself, and start building a safe place to regain my strength and figure out what the hell happened over the last 20 years.

Being freed from the toxic cocoon of my marriage gave me a new perspective that showed me clearly just how constrained, criticized, controlled and manipulated I had become. I started gaining awareness that although I had for decades believed I was comfortable and in a happy relationship (at the amusement park of distraction), I had actually been being slowly smothered to death with self-denial and constriction. Beyond the troubled aspects of my marriage, I was starving for deep connection and spirituality, and did not know it. Years later, I now understand that the issues being raised in my marriage were an invitation to soul-level healing and personal growth. The marriage was simply reflecting back to me all the places

I was unhealed. But I was scared to admit that things were going wrong. Being a child of divorce, it was so important to me to succeed at my marriage that I ignored evidence of trouble until it nearly drove me mad. As with most major changes in life, when the suffering is great enough we make the change that has been demanded by our souls. In the end I could finally witness the harness that bound me, and I was glad to be free of it.

Although I was relieved to be autonomous, floating in absolute sovereignty felt scary to me. I was used to such tightly controlled parameters that when I broke out of my prison, I felt agoraphobic standing in the middle of a wide open field of possibility. I wanted to feel the safety of that other half. I wanted to cling to a life preserver to keep me from drowning in self-governance on the brink of potential bad decisions that could cascade dramatically into radical failure. I was afraid without my cocoon. I doubted my own strength because I never felt it before; I was always 'We,' enmeshed so intrinsically with my other half that in many areas I did not know where he started and I began. I had been so daring and independent within the context of my marriage because I felt the foundation of 'We.' Now that it was 'Me,' I felt like a good gust of wind could probably sweep me quickly into destitution. It was a completely irrational fear, but it was omnipresent.

So the interviewing process began with an endless stream of men who, truth be told, didn't really want to audition for the part of Everything Man.

Seeking another 'We'

If you have spent the majority of your life in a 'We' construct, it makes perfect sense that being single might feel frightening and lonely. It makes sense that you might want to immediately find a replacement for the spouse you lost so that you can, once again, become part of a 'We.'

Warning: if you've been in a long-term relationship, things have changed since your last date. You and your contemporaries are older and have been through a helluva journey and typically everyone has lots of baggage. People that remained single the whole time have had a really different journey than you. Society has shifted in how it communicates and connects; for example, texting was new for me in the dating context since it was invented near the end of my marriage. And you probably need to rediscover yourself at this phase of your life due to having forgotten who you were while simultaneously having grown into a new person that you don't yet know.

The human marketplace (or, dating at 40)

Remember when you were a child and you played secret games with your closest friend, making up rules on-the-fly with near-telekinetic understandings as the game changed and rules were dynamically altered to fit the new conditions? Now remember a time when a different friend came to play and was completely frustrated at trying to understand all the mysterious conventions concocted in the magical world created by you and your best friend. Welcome to dating after being married for two decades. No one understands your game because they weren't there creating it with you. In fact, they've been busy immersed in their own realities, making up rules of the game with various lovers, or living independently and single-handedly building entire infrastructures defining the 'way it is.'

The first thing I noticed upon entering the dating world again was that there were a lot of men on the dating site. It was dial-a-man online shopping. I could even streamline by only viewing men that had the specific features I desired. At first I thought this was going to be easy; I can just place my order online and request delivery by Saturday. Unfortunately, shopping for men is not nearly as predictable as buying clothing online (and that, my friends, is unpredictable).

People are often mistaken about their identities when creating their own profile pages. I'm not sure it's *lying* per se, but it is most definitely not accurate much of the time. Crafting a genuine profile page requires that you actually know yourself and are honest about what you see in the mirror. It also requires that you are not pretending to be someone you are not (even to yourself).

When I was writing my first profile page, I realized I had no idea of how to describe myself to others. I had not needed to explain who I was to anyone in a really, really long time. I also felt a highly uncomfortable sensation as I emerged into the light without a darkness to push against; I had defined 'Me' within the context of 'We' for so long that I did not know how to explain 'Me' within a 'Me' context. I was also extremely insecure about presenting myself to the world, and worried about exposing all the shame/guilt/unworthiness I felt from my rebellious choices at the end of my marriage. Over the months and years I wrote, revised, edited, drafted and redrafted my profile page to fit the new 'Me' as I evolved, and to attempt to appeal to the sort of man I wanted to attract at each phase of my rebirth. As a writer, and a person intent on conveying my authentic self to others, I worked tirelessly on my profile page; in the end, I realized my profile page was a labor of cultivating self-love and understanding.

Many of the disappointments early in my dating life after divorce were due to my unconscious and incorrect belief that I knew the impeccable way to behave in a relationship. More accurate is that I knew extremely well how to behave in my marriage. And because I clung to the game I knew, I judged many men harshly for not knowing how to play by my 'We' rules.

After years of dating, a lot of personal development, and studying awareness practices and *The Four Agreements* by Don Miguel Ruiz, I now understand that every person has a unique world view that informs their perceptions and influences their actions. The more mature we are, the more experiences we have had that support our conclusions (since the Universe reflects to us according to our perceptions), and the less malleable we are when having a relationship negotiation—especially if we are living unconsciously.

Increase resiliency with relationships by:

- Staying conscious in the present moment (rather than drifting off into the Netherland of the past).
- Maintaining awareness that there are many right answers and you have a unique perspective (unlikely to be shared by another completely).
- Listening and hearing what another person is saying with curiosity and an open mind. Asking lots of questions and listening to the answers.
- Communicating your own perceptions and beliefs clearly.
- Realizing that whatever is making you unhappy about the other person is more than likely a wound within yourself that needs healing.

It is extremely unlikely to ever find a person that knows how to play the game the way you created it with your ex. It's more realistic to let go of the old game, and start inventing a new one. After all, that game didn't work out and you didn't want to play it anymore anyways.

Dismantling the old game and stepping out of outdated roles and agreements is a process because it requires self-awareness to spot those unconscious aspects of self, and then it takes dedication and fearlessness to let go and step into something new and unknown. The rebirthing process happens in layers. The deeper the layers of past-unconscious-pretense that you extricate from yourself, and the more effort you put into consciously crafting a belief system of your choosing, the longer-lasting and more deeply satisfying your life will eventually become because you will truly be living it as YOU want to.

All that being said, here are some pitfalls I ran into when dating again after so much time in a committed relationship:

- Married people. I have known some divorcees who found it acceptable to have sex with married people. Personally, this arrangement does not fulfill me. I fell into this situation unintentionally a couple of times; in one instance, I cultivated feelings for a man who had no intention of leaving his wife. It was very difficult for me to handle this arrangement emotionally. Having feelings for someone who is committed in a love relationship to someone else involves you in an ethical triangle, generally means secret communication, and invites the possibility of retaliation from the person's spouse. While you're not the one 'cheating,' you are most certainly enabling the cheating to occur. Married people do not always come out and admit they are married. A sign that the person you are dating might be married is that the person does not return communications from you during certain timeframes (i.e., when they are likely with their spouse), does not invite you over to his/her home, and is hesitant about making plans in advance. Facebook is a wonderful research tool when determining the relationship status of a person you are dating, as well as asking lots of questions and keeping track of the answers.

- Hot and heavy. Having jumped right into the deep end of the pool a number of times, I can safely say that fast-paced, intense romantic liaisons are generally short-lived. The end goal of intense romantic liaisons is usually either sex or recreation of the 'We' cocoon in that Poppy Field of disillusion we discussed already. Towards this end, your dating partner will strive to build instant intimacy so that the warm, oozy feelings of cuddle time or gazing into one another's eyes will quickly lead to passion, or to the sensation of being in a long-term relationship without going through the long-term part. There are people addicted to the intoxicating feelings brought on by romance and sexual pursuit. It's fun at first. And then it's not so easy once the real personalities start emerging and breaking through the fantasies. It can be very disappointing when reality is a far cry from the amazing illusion you created in your mind about who you were dating. Choose the tortoise. Slow and steady wins the race.

- Differences in attachment styles. After three years of dating essentially the same man, I finally was directed to *Attached: The New Science of Adult Attachment and How It Can Help You Find - and Keep - Love* by Amir Levine and Rachel Heller. This book very helpfully explained that there are different styles of intimate attachment, and that not all of those styles are compatible. For example, if you are a person that prefers a lot of regular communication, and you're dating someone who can go a week without responding to you, chances are this is a match that will drive you bonkers. Figuring out your personal attachment style, and then being prepared with the knowledge you need to select an appropriate partner, will save you a lot of time and heartache.

Most of all, no matter how a person behaves while dating you, *do not take it personally*. How a person behaves is how that person behaves, whether in relation to you or someone else. What can be interesting, however, is to notice where you are triggered. When you are dating someone, are there things they do or say that affect your mood, make you question yourself, or otherwise bother you? In my experience, these are the spiritual lessons to be gleaned from seeing the mirror of ourselves reflected back to us via this other person. For example, my ex-husband was often critical of me during our marriage; this was a mirror of how I was internally (consciously and unconsciously) critical of myself. He was doing to me on the outside what I was doing to myself on the inside. This is what I mean by relationships often being 'mirrors' for unhealed aspects of ourselves.

I've learned a lot by paying attention to mirrors and doing personal inquiry into the shadow aspects of myself that are brought forth by these reflections. Part of my operating theory is that the resonance of my energy and unconscious/conscious beliefs is attracting to me another person who is vibrating on my same wavelength, so to speak. I have studied the Law of Attraction and leveraged it to manifest desired outcomes by elevating my energy through personal healing, and projecting clear intention and vision. Each time I have manifested a new lover, I notice how the curve of elevation and higher vibration is maintained in the personality, energy, and positivity of the person connected to me. In other words, whoever I am dating is reflecting my current state of being to me as I evolve and ascend towards more authentic expression of myself. It can be very illuminating seeing one's current spiritual progress through the mirror of another person.

Battling instant response syndrome

Coming from a highly co-dependent relationship, I was accustomed to expect an instant response from my ex-husband whenever I would text or call him, and vice versa. In the early days of our relationship, response was expected within an hour or two of a phone message to work or home. When we adopted cell phones, that response time shrank to a fraction of an hour. As we began having trouble in our relationship, the cell phone noose tightened as distrust grew. Near the end, my ex-husband would simply call my cellphone repeatedly until I picked up.

I loathed being on a cellphone leash, and yet it was strangely comforting at the same time. I think it must be similar to how convicts feel when they are freed from jail—something in them yearns for the familiarity of the cage.

My initial forays into dating proved that I had been conditioned by my boundary-less marriage to expect instant response to my messages from every person in my life: especially a person I was dating. When I started dating Z shortly after the ending of my marriage, I did not realize that my expectations were out of line. Like a frog in a pot of water that had been slowly heated to boiling, it never occurred to me that I could be freely jumping around on lily pads in a wide-open pond. I certainly did not want to give another person that freedom—the freedom to respond to my message whenever they wanted to—because that threatened my sense of wellbeing by questioning the very structure under which I had been living my life for twenty years. I mean, I might *die* if my beloved did not respond to me within minutes.

Z had been single for most of his life, except for a five-year period during which he tried marriage. He was accustomed to a lot of freedom. He liked to leave his cellphone at home and go wandering around during his free time away from work. He was free and he was not about to be yoked by my cellphone noose into instant response servitude.

What Z did not understand is that his refusal to slip my noose around his neck meant that I had to actually deal with myself, and what had become a completely unreasonable, anxiety-ridden system of coping in a relationship. When he would view my message, and not respond, my anxiety would shoot through the roof and activate my very capable inner judge in launching fear missiles throughout my brain. The frustration and anger triggered by this viewing-and-not-responding would make me want to lash out.

The more Z would not respond to my messages, the more desperate for his response I would become; a negative response was better than no response. It was a vicious cycle. I now understand that the pattern is identified as the dynamic between an 'anxious attachment' person and an 'avoidant attachment' person. (Read *"Attached: The New Science of Adult Attachment and How It Can Help You Find - and Keep - Love"* by Amir Levine and Rachel Heller for more information.)

Nonetheless, I soon realized I had a lot of personal work to do to untangle the compulsory response system that had defined my relationship communication strategy for the better part of my adult life. First step was to silence my inner judge who would rear her ugly head whenever a response was not forthcoming. Second step was to learn to sit through discomfort and simply witness it. Third step was to put my attention on the 'now' in my own life whenever I found it outside of myself.

Over the course of dating and doing my personal work for several years, I have been able to go without a response from a lover for up to a week without having a serious reaction. And now that I have been able to come to terms with my need for instant response, I find myself in relationship with people who freely respond to my communications within a very cordial timeframe.

Silencing the inner judge

Part of what caused distress whenever a lover was not responding to my message was a vast undercurrent of very negative thoughts in my subconscious mind. I became aware of these thoughts because I was doing intensive personal work to expand my 'awareness.' I not only heard these negative thoughts, but also became aware of subconscious beliefs, internal agreements, and behavior patterns that were unproductive. I was studying *The Four Agreements* by Don Miguel Ruiz and learning about the Inner Judge who casts down dictates in the form of rules by which I should live (rules that often conflicted with one another), as well as judgments about my personal character and how well I lived by the 'rules.' The judgments coursing through my mind had the sole purpose of undercutting my self-worth and confidence. The vicious thoughts would spur hurtful stories in my conscious mind to explain why my lover was not responding.

"He's with another woman."

"He doesn't care about you."

"He doesn't respect you. If he did, he'd respond."

Once I realized my mind was intentionally trying to concoct stories to hurt me or make me push away a lover, I decided to do something about it. I wrote down all the hurtful stories on paper so I could see them in black and white. The interesting thing about looking at the shadows, or the things hurting us in our subconscious, is that it becomes clearer that the thoughts are untrue when you see them in the light, or with your conscious mind.

After witnessing these thoughts, I then used the element of fire to assist me in eliminating these thoughts from my being. I took the paper with the hurtful story written on it into my hands. I closed my eyes and felt in my body how this story made me feel inside. I pulled up that yucky feeling from my body using my in-breath, and blew it out of my body and into the paper with my out-breath. In this way, I transferred the hurtful feelings from my body into the paper. Then, I set the paper on fire to release the story and the bad feelings it caused.

Lastly, I picked up a journal and wrote a new story for myself. I had to distance myself from association with my brain. The brain is a servant, it's a computer: you are the master, the programmer of your brain. I needed strong methods of refocusing my attention to drive the point home to my brain. I wrote each new agreement 13 times in a journal. Why 13 times? It reinforces the new agreement through writing by hand, and it sends a clear message to the brain: *"Change the belief. I am in charge of what you believe, not you."* (And no...typing the agreement on a computer or iPad is not the same as writing it by hand on paper.)

Does it matter whether the story was 'true'? Not really. In the moment, without communication from the lover, I did not know the 'truth' anyway. All that matters in this moment is supporting yourself with a story that helps you, rather than harms you.

"I don't know what he is doing right now."

"I am worthy of respect."

"I care for myself."

Using this process, I retrained my brain away from telling pointless stories, and encouraged myself to adopt new agreements that I could actually control—my relationship with myself.

So you might ask how many licks are there to the center of the tootsie roll pop? How many times do you have to do this burning paper routine to change your mind? Well, it's up to you. The only thing you have to do is persevere until the persistent undesirable urge/thought/pattern actually *changes*.

Relationship via text

A dynamic I have noticed over the last several years of dating is the strategy of conducting a relationship via text messaging. I was using this strategy unconsciously for several years, and then woke up one day and realized something significant: texting someone is not being in a relationship with them. (*duh*)

Putting a screen between you and another person—like texting or online dating—adds emotional distance that clearly serves as a self-protection strategy. You think you are 'getting to know' someone because you are texting them and they are texting you. You can keep the relationship going on the back burner without using a lot of flame, but simply making quick remarks like 'lol' and 'how was your day' and 'good night' and 'muah.' This interaction is comforting when you feel lonely because it makes you feel like someone cares about you. Keeping the interactions to primarily text means you do not have to invest much of yourself, you get attention to feel special, and you feel safe because you can always just choose not to respond to a text message if a person upsets you or you get bored. You can even click Delete or Block and instantly remove this person from your life, which streamlines breaking up so you can feel less awkward and guilty about it.

The problem is this: texting as the primary vehicle for communication is not having a relationship. Texting denies humanity its natural desire for physical contact, hearing the intonations and vibration of speech, watching facial expressions, making eye contact, and generally being in the person's presence. Holding hands, hugging, kissing and being touched is necessary for cultivating intimacy in a relationship. You can only touch a person when you're physically in proximity with that person. If you're only using texting to conduct your relationship, you're missing out on the gold, the gems, and the diamonds.

Perhaps while you are recovering your self-esteem following your divorce it makes sense to keep several people texting you to help you see your good qualities and make yourself feel better. Just be aware that texting as a means of relationship communication is not effective, and will eventually need to be abandoned in favor of in-person communication. Consider the people that are your best friends—how did you build the relationship with these people? Did you build a relationship with them using text messaging? More than likely, your closest friends spent time with you in person and shared experiences which created the friendship relationship. Perhaps you text your friends, but it is only a part of the communication that takes place between you. Dating works the same way.

Dating to disguise inner lack

Constantly texting with multiple lovers or endlessly searching dating sites is a way to get attention and create a level of distraction that helps you forget your current life situation and how it makes you feel. When I left my marriage I spent countless hours scanning dating profiles, sending flirt messages, and texting back and forth with various men who lived all over the United States (except where I lived). I wanted the attention, I did not want to feel lonely, and I was operating under the illusion that somewhere out there was a magical person that would make me feel loved and appreciated and *then* I would be happy. The fact that most of the men I dated lived remote was a significant factor in my self-delusion because I could imagine them to be anyone I wanted without reality getting in the way.

At a certain point I noticed that a deeper connection was not present in all that busyness, and that the loneliness was still inside of me untouched. Also, whenever I started to expand interaction with a man beyond surface-level texting, in an attempt to fill my loneliness with external attention, inevitably the man did not respond in the way I wanted (because he wasn't actually the person I was imagining him to be) and I was left feeling the full brunt of my submerged discomfort.

The only way truly past the loneliness is to stop running from it, and get comfortable with it. Only by sitting through the discomfort can we dispel it from our lives at last, and move forward into new possibilities. When we face the discomfort, and allow ourselves to feel it fully, the fear of experiencing the discomfort is vanquished and we become emotionally stronger and more present with ourselves. From this place of strength and presence it is easier to avoid the disappointments that are usually part of the dating process because you can enter a dating situation fully conscious and ready to experience what *IS* without attachment to the outcome. Going through a period of celibacy where you do not participate in the dating process is key to getting past loneliness (see **Reclaiming self through celibacy**). Rather than running from the loneliness or submerging it or masking it, *lean into* the loneliness to get past it.

It is true that when you decide you are ready for a new relationship, there is a certain amount of busyness from dating that is necessary as you get to know different people to determine if there is a match. The way to tell whether the pursuit of dating is to distract yourself or to find a partner is to observe your focus and reaction to the dating. Are you willing to be present right from the first date with the actual person in front of you, and walk away if there is not a suitable match? Or do you persist in communication even when you know there is not a match just because you don't want to be without that small measure of comfort you receive from interacting with that person?

Our boldness with the catch and release of dating has everything to do with how we derive our happiness. If our happiness is the result of a direct connection to Source and self-acceptance and love, and it bubbles up from within us no matter what is happening around us, then releasing someone who does not match your relationship preferences does not affect the stability of your happiness.

Cheating on the flip side

On the single side of the extra-marital affair triangle, what I experienced was different than when I was the married woman cheating on my husband. I was not the person who had made a promise to be monogamous with another individual. At the time, I was single and feeling lonely, and the love feeling, the passion, that this married man was able to give me was intoxicating. It was almost as if I was able to sample the marital cocoon and all its assurance and safety, without actually being in the marital agreement. Being in proximity to the marital cocoon felt comforting in my world where I was adrift alone on a little raft in a vast ocean. His presence allowed me to plunge the depths of my imaginary world where he was my husband.

The only problem of course, was that he was not my husband. I wanted what I could not have, and soon the feelings of lack and jealousy took over and left me feeling depressed every time he would leave me and go home to his wife. Of course, I also felt guilt at having enabled his cheating, but more than that, I felt abandoned and alone. "Why can't I have a guy like that all to myself?" I questioned. The inevitable answer was "You're not good enough." I was back at square one from the other side of the proposition.

After this initial affair with a married man, I avoided married men at all costs, so painful was my disillusion. As luck would have it, I was deceived a few times afterwards by men who claimed to be single but then turned out, in fact, to be married. One of these men sent me into a nearly irrepressible rage upon discovering his true relationship status. It can be a very frustrating feeling to know what you do not want, and then to be deceived into experiencing it again. I began to learn that Spirit will test your resolve when you choose the righteous path you intend to follow.

Reflecting upon all these experiences from my current vantage point, I see from a larger perspective how our society has created constructs that are nearly impossible to achieve (until death do us part) while simultaneously filling us with messages of lack and scarcity to create a profound longing—along with the message that our longing is fulfilled from sex, alcohol, and material wealth. I have only been able to witness this larger perspective because during my healing journey I stepped out of the collective dream and turned inwards; inside of myself I found my own voice, my own wisdom, and my own beliefs. More than that, I found the Source that dwells inside all beings, and this discovery has led to inner peace, self-acceptance, compassion, and love. It has been an arduous intense journey, but I no longer *need* another person to fulfill me (although I *desire* human connection). I am no longer willing to sell myself on the human marketplace in exchange for fleeting acceptance and passion. My soul is not for sale.

What happens when a person loves herself/himself is that the compulsory addictive desires lessen immeasurably and eventually disappear. Finding a love partner becomes a matter of preference rather than the elixir of life. From self-love, it is quite simple to avoid complex love triangles or relationships that lack integrity.

From my current vantage point, I am also able to witness how simply being truthful and non-judgmental about your desires can lead to a new relationship framework that is authentic, allows personal freedom, and rewards radical honesty. The pull of the traditional love relationship is an energetic force that can be felt across our society and is very strong; however there are people who are building other models of relationship based on their own truths and clear interpersonal agreements, and experiencing love with freedom that respects the authenticity of the individuals agreeing to the relationship parameters. The necessary ingredients to the new relationship models are a willingness to claim personal responsibility for your thoughts/beliefs/perceptions/actions, a strong effort at clear communication that includes plenty of witnessing and listening, and a focus on conscious participation that does not take things personally and leaves the inner and outer judges behind.

The herpes discussion

Right before I met my husband, I had moved out to San Francisco alone following college to start my first job as a technical writer in the Bay Area. In the three weeks I was living in San Francisco, I had sex with my roommate, who was sleeping with our other roommate, and managed to contract genital herpes. I had gone from a high school and college steady boyfriend, to three weeks of freedom and with one sexual encounter—I forever changed my sexual life.

Many people have huge misconceptions about herpes. Once I was sitting in a women's circle and the subject came up for discussion about dating and sex and STDs, and pretty soon the fear was as thick as molasses, clinging in the air like a rank sweaty fog. Finally, I raised my hand and offered some actual truth to dispel the incredible amount of misinformation that was rapid-firing around the room.

Herpes is the ostrich with its head in the sand in this country. According to the CDC, in 2014 at least 26% of people 40-49 in the U.S. have been medically diagnosed with the genital type of herpes. Standard STD tests do not test for herpes, and so even this figure is outrageously shy of the potential statistics in a population that does not talk about herpes, does not test for herpes, and pretends that they don't have herpes. Many people are completely clueless they have herpes because it is so innocuous. Almost the entire population has the strain of herpes that causes cold sores in your mouth—you get that when grandma kisses you as a baby. And yet the public at large wants to ostracize anyone who confesses to having herpes because they are so afraid of catching it and having their entire life 'ruined.' My ex-husband routinely told me "We can't leave each other now because we're damaged goods and no one will want us."

The only thing in my life ruined by herpes was the treatment and perception I received from misinformed and undereducated people. Living with herpes (for me) was like living any other day as a human being in good health. Dating with herpes presented the challenge of communicating the truth and being ready to receive whatever reaction comes your way. I learned that I did not want to tell a man before he had a chance to meet me because it is easy to reject someone for herpes without taking time to get to know them. I also did not want to wait too long to tell a man because the more feelings you have for someone, the more it hurts if they choose to walk away. Picking the moment to tell someone can be tricky; honestly, there is never a good time.

Using protection during sex and taking anti-viral medication like Valtrex helped me to not 'give' it to anyone I had sex with over the course of dating, except for my ex-husband with whom I started having sex right after infection (the most infectious time) and one man I dated who indicated he believed I had given it to him. Statistically, my personal experience showed very low odds of spreading it during intercourse with the precautions I took. Apparently there is also a vaccination to prevent a woman from catching herpes, if they currently do not have it (not a vaccine for men currently).

Although having herpes was challenging, no challenges in life come without gifts. The gifts I received from herpes include:

- A built-in mechanism for determining which men were serious about dating me as a whole person, and which men only wanted to have sex with me. While there certainly were those cases of men in denial when standing in front of the candy counter, for the most part the herpes discussion brought a level of seriousness into play for most men I dated. Being with me required a conscious choice, and at some level that felt good every time the answer was 'Yes.'

- Experiencing how terrible shame and guilt feel when you do not speak your truth. There was about a year where I chose not to tell lovers that I had herpes. I took my medicine and I used protection and avoided sex if I felt I had an active outbreak—but I did not give the man the benefit of choice. This approach led me to feel lower and lower self-esteem, and taught me a valuable lesson about shame and its impact on self-worth. Once I started confessing the truth to each lover, going back through my rolodex up to a year prior, I felt lighter and lighter. The truth indeed sets you free, and I was able to experience it because of my herpes challenge.

- Learning first-hand about how fear can cause people to alienate others; and when you experience the 'worst thing that can happen,' it liberates you to love with your whole heart. Now that I have felt rejection because of a physical challenge, I have immense compassion for others whose bodies keep them from living as fully, and connecting as freely with others, as their hearts desire. I have compassion for people who are told they will live constrained or ill the 'rest of their lives.' And I have a passion to help others change their DNA through energy medicine and the power of intention.

- Experiencing the impact of stress and anxiety on the body, and the amazing benefit of meditation, grounding, and calming yourself. If I hadn't contracted herpes, I might not have realized how my anxiety and high stress was punishing my body. But with herpes, each time I let my anxiety and stress get out of control, my body warned me. Working with this virus, I learned the importance of letting go, tuning out, and finding inner peace. I learned how to maintain equilibrium and peace so that my body could have a healthy response to my life.

When your ex gets a new lover

When I left my marriage, I told my husband *"There's someone for you to love. Someone who will fill your heart with joy. I promise...you will be so much happier with someone different than me."*

As time passed, we each moved into new phases of our lives, navigating what parts of our experiences or personalities or beliefs were authentic to our unique selves, and what parts had to be left behind during the process of dissolving the union that lived for over twenty years. We each grew, experimented with loving other people, lived afresh the intense/joyful/aching experience of dating; this time as much older adults than the twenty-somethings that met and fell in love.

Fully anticipated, yet surprising all the same, the moment finally came when I realized that the prediction I made years ago had come true: my ex-husband had fallen in love with a new woman. A range of feelings passed over me during this dawning realization, each one prompting investigation into the inner workings of my heart and mind. Anger that he had introduced this woman to my parents and children. Jealousy that she had been giving my sons hand-written notes and thoughtful gifts. Self-pity that I did not have someone to love, too. All of this emotional sludge was gunking up the works, causing uncomfortable and toxic interactions with my ex-husband.

My time spent on the spiritual path was helpful in providing me the essential awareness that prompted these questions:

we had a bond that transcended our marriage

What are you holding onto? And why are you holding onto it?

I dove deep into these questions, tracking the energetics that needed to be released, and then did the energetic healing to release it. I worked a sand painting, moving my ex-husband out of my family circle. I had a friend perform an energy healing for me to release the marriage, to let it go—the good, the bad, the indifferent. I cut the cords–AGAIN–from my ex-husband, severing the bonds between us. I burned a big beautiful photograph from our wedding, releasing the marriage with gratitude for all the love and experiences shared. I participated in a Despacho service with a Q'ero shaman who was passing through town, and gave gratitude for the gifts of the marriage; especially my two wonderful sons, my greatest creations.

The gift of freedom from my past finally arrived in a completely unexpected way: Facebook. Someone had posted the story of Brenda Schmitz, a woman who passed away from ovarian cancer two years previous, but planned ahead at her death to give her husband permission to love again, to move forward with his life. She wrote a wish list for the local radio station, and asked a friend to send it when her husband fell in love again. As one of her three wishes, she asked that the listeners of the radio station send her husband's new love a day of pampering. Brenda wanted to honor this woman's efforts in loving her children, when she couldn't be there.

In that moment of reading Brenda's wishes, I realized my heart could open and embrace and appreciate my ex-husband's girlfriend. In that moment, I remembered how much I loved this man, enough to say 'I do,' and I remembered I wanted him to be happy. In that moment, I found gratitude that my ex-husband chose to love someone who was kind, generous, and thoughtful; and who treated my children as one of her own. In that moment, I became free of my past by embracing the present.

72

Looking in the mirror and facing shadows

At a certain point I wondered if I was a sadist because I would keep getting back up after being knocked down by the dating game. Voices in my head would shout 'Stay down, stay down!' But participating in these relationships seemed to be my way of seeing my wounded self that needed healing, and later, the healed aspects of self that were emerging. At many points, engaging in relationship became a measure of how far I had come in my spiritual growth. I became very open to the idea that the behavior or attitudes I saw in the other person were a projection of the healing that needed to take place within myself. I came to see that, without a doubt, these men were being sent with a message; all I had to do was be willing to witness and claim it, thereby unlocking another layer to my healing.

"We see the world not as it is, but as we are." — *Anais Nin*

We have all met someone who 'triggers' us, who we dislike immediately and push away with criticism and judgment. Those qualities we are repulsed by are, at a deeply denied level, qualities we possess ourselves that lurk in our shadow self. For example, I can be triggered by people who insist they know the one right way to do something. What bothers me about this is how it denies me of having a way to do that 'something' that is different and still valid. This need to be right is a deep shadow part of myself of which I am aware. When I discover a shadow aspect of myself, the work is to loosen and dissolve it by understanding what feeds that aspect of self, and finding a more positive way to nourish and strengthen myself. In this case, the work is to continue to gently redirect myself towards self-validation and trusting my own intuition.

In rare cases, you meet a life-size mirror of yourself so that you can fully experience yourself as others do. During the course of dating I had the honor of meeting such a mirror, and while the experience was intense, it was also extremely validating and insightful. Through interaction with my mirror, I was able to fully experience my former wounded self—the self who made assumptions, who took things personally, who could not respect boundaries, and who did not love myself (even though I thought I did at the time!). My mirror enabled me to feel the effects of my former self from my newer, more healed self; I could feel my old self's powerful desire to be loved and accepted along with my former loneliness, rejection, hopelessness, and general yuckiness when the object of my desire did not reciprocate. Overwhelming feelings of compassion for my former self and my mirror mixed with gratitude for the journey that has led me to a more healed state where love and acceptance do not need to come from outside of myself. I have now stood on both sides of this mirror: I have compassion for my former self and how I struggled inside myself to feel worthy of love, and at the same time I finally understand how and why my longing and desperate need for love pushed away the very person whose attention I craved. I finally know how it felt to be the target of my powerful needs. Because of this experience, I know without a doubt that I have significantly healed along my journey, and I know the kind of lover I wish to be in the future. While it is always a difficult situation when two people part ways, it was with gratitude that I waved goodbye to my mirror; he was a very significant teacher, allowing me to come full circle to truly understand the journey I have undertaken.

So as you walk through life and come across people that make you react—in a positive or negative way—take a moment and consider: what is this person reflecting to me about myself? Looking into the mirror is a powerful way to learn and grow.

Projections and being a victim

When you start dating again a dangerous pitfall is to project onto a new person the traits of your former spouse. I dated a man as I was writing this book who told me that most of the serious relationships in his life had been with Cancer women, and none of them had worked out. As it turns out, I am a Cancer woman. Receiving his early assessment of our potential based on my astrological sign insulted me because it insinuated that I am, somehow, not a unique person; that I am an exact replica of every other woman who is a

Cancer. When we project our own stuff from past relationships onto a new person we deny them their individuality and specialness, and we decide up front it is not going to work (which becomes a self-fulfilling prophesy).

When a person's reactions do not match the reality of interactions with you, it is quite possible that there are mental projections at work. If we are not consciously aware that our minds project onto other people qualities based on our own perceptions and beliefs, we can feel very certain that what we think about the other person is 'true' and can find plenty of supporting evidence (even if a balanced view reveals the opposite).

You can easily lose amazing opportunities with incredible people if you are unconscious to your mind's projections. Just because your former spouse liked to watch football on Sunday and drank too much beer and got violent with you, does not mean that every man who watches football on Sunday drinks too much beer and resorts to violence against women. *my mom didn't love me enough Jack " " "*

So if mind projections are damaging to us, why do we allow them to exist? Because if we can point the finger at someone else for why the relationship is not working out, we can become a victim and be absolved of our personal responsibility and we don't have to change. If we are caught in a 'trap' of dating the same person again and again—these damn Cancer women that expect too much of us—then we are poor, defenseless victims of fate (or astrology) that are doing absolutely nothing to provoke a failing relationship.

The way out of mental projections is to claim personal responsibility for your part of a relationship, and to stay absolutely present and observant to what is *actually* happening with interactions for *this* relationship in *this* moment. Heraclitus in Ancient Greece said *"No man ever steps in the same river twice, for it's not the same river and he's not the same man."* If we are doing our personal work, and learning from our mistakes, then we are never the same person from moment to moment. And as life is constantly changing, our environment (the river) is also never the same from moment to moment. So when we come to cross the river (face a recurring challenge), our response has the potential to be different every time we stick a toe in the water if we can bring the light of our awareness and consciousness to the present situation.

My mind wants to project positive attributes onto every person I date; this is something I have learned about myself by being willing to be a witness to my patterns. So in this case, I ran an experiment without attachment to the outcome to see whether what I thought was happening was *actually* happening. I got a very clear answer in rapid time, and I acted on it to break out of my own projection pattern. I saw this man for who he truly was in that moment, and realized that I was spending a lot of time trying to force the attention of a man who was not ready for a serious relationship. Rather than letting myself remain a victim to my mental projections that were leading me to experience rejection rather than connection, I took responsibility for my own mental projection, became present and curious, ran an experiment, witnessed the truth with the light of my own consciousness, and took appropriate action to revise my expectations. A shorter way of saying this is I stopped banging my head against a brick wall. His behavior had nothing to do with my worth as a person, or my viability as a woman in a relationship. We were simply at different places in the current moment, and I had a choice of whether to continue engaging with the dynamic.

Fully embracing 'Me'

At some point in my dating frenzy, a part of me stepped outside of myself and began to witness the cyclical patterns unfolding in my relationship dramas. I was exhausted with scouring the dating sites for a man, falling fast and hard in a romantic daze, spending hours talking and getting to know each other, waking to the dawning realization that he was not going to work out, and signing back onto the dating sites. Pouring my heart and soul into every new man I met over the Internet was draining my emotional resources at a breakneck pace.

The messages started sinking in when the fifth mentor suggested I try being alone for a while. The last thing I wanted to do was to be alone. In my perception, being 'alone' was the same as being 'lonely.' If I didn't have a man dedicated to me in a monogamous relationship there must be something wrong with me. Where was that knight in shining armor that was supposed to rescue me after I left my marriage?

What finally made me stop the dating merry-go-round was pure emotional exhaustion that I could not ignore, and not overcome, without taking a break. For the first time since I hit puberty, I was ready to try being alone.

I did not hold steady with being alone in one long drawn-out period. It was more like a pendulum. At first I was alone for several weeks (which felt like an eternity), and then I dove back into dating. Over time, I extended the gap of not dating into months. I started to notice that my self-esteem and self-reliance rose in direct proportion to the time I spent in the not-dating gap. I started to become aware that when I was dating a man, I slipped into an alter ego version of myself who hid her light under a bushel, morphed into a person compatible with the current man, and daydreamed for hours fantasizing romantic encounters and wedding vows.

The final straw was when I discerned that I was changing myself to be acceptable to a man, and that I was living in my imagination rather than in reality. This behavioral pattern was completely at odds with the career and life intentions I set for myself to become a transformation coach and energy medicine practitioner who helps other people shift their repeating patterns. It was time for a change. It was time to face my greatest fear: *loneliness.*

Sitting through the discomfort of loneliness

In the early days of transition to being single, I would often experience panic and anxiety triggered by the lack of the marital cocoon. Trying to suppress this fear with alcohol didn't work. Trying to recreate the semblance of a marital cocoon by roping a lover into my instant response servitude didn't work. Wanting to run away was pointless; I did not want to leave my kids in the home alone. Eventually there was only one thing left to do—face the fear of loneliness.

An amazing thing happens when you allow the waves of anxiety, fear, sadness, and anger to pass over you: they pass. Usually within a few minutes. Resisting these feelings is what prolongs them. But if you can simply trust that they will pass in a few minutes, and allow them to wash over you without resistance, you will dissolve them much more quickly. During the process of facing your feelings, remember that anything your mind tells you is absolutely suspect as complete falsehood. The good news is that as you become aware of your internal stories and beliefs, your mind starts to get a lot quieter because it learns that you mean business, and you will dismiss its concoctions as soon as they are revealed.

For a time I adopted a practice of sitting in my dark closet to face my feelings. I would sit in the pitch-black and let the feelings wash over me without resistance; once peace descended, I would languish in that state for a while and then return to life.

The more often you survive these experiences of *feeling*, the more courage you have to face your truth at deeper and deeper levels. This process heals you, strengthens you, and transforms you. I have learned that Spirit never gives a person more than she can handle.

At some point when you are spiritually ready to face it, a penetrating loneliness may descend periodically. When this profound loneliness would come over me it would trigger anger followed by acute sadness and tears. Early on, I released the tension of this loneliness by blaming and telling stories about what this person or that did to me to make this unbearable aching in my body happen. Over time, I learned to be with the intense distress until it passed and endure it without acting out or spinning stories. I learned that if I could be present with the pain, I could get to the other side and where the relief was like a breath of fresh air. Peace with myself and acceptance of the current state of my life without struggling to make it different.

Turning inwards and opening to Spirit

Incessant mental chatter that repeats the same anxious thoughts over and over, music or television or news playing constantly in the background, talking all day about problems over the phone—all of this internal and external noise prevents a clear channel to guidance and clarity from Spirit (or however you envision the consciousness that surrounds and indwells us). Only when our minds are silent, and our BEings are experiencing peace, does clarity arise.

Facing silence can be uncomfortable because all the things our mind is doing to avoid silence, it is doing because it is covering up whatever it is we are afraid to know about ourselves. A lot of what our mind is hiding from us, however, is not truth; it is simply a story we unconsciously concocted about ourselves based on false agreements made throughout our lives. I am lonely. No one is there. No one wants to be w/ me.

When I sat in the dark in my closet and faced my fears, I listened to these stories. Placing the light of my awareness on these stories dissolved their power because once my conscious mind discovered what I was telling myself subconsciously, I was able to release these negative stories as false, and write new stories for myself that were supportive and loving. Loving yourself is a long process of witnessing your thoughts, beliefs and behavior, and gently and compassionately redirecting yourself.

The spiritual journey opens your channel to Spirit by removing all the blockages placed in that channel throughout your life to prevent you from seeing your own truth. The journey is ultimately to raise your essential self to the surface of your being, and allow that self to chart the course of your life. During the journey you release the false selves—the roles you took on to please other people, the beliefs you adopted because you were trained in these thoughts by your parents or community, and the behaviors you habituated to cope with your life. Only by fearlessly questioning everything you think you 'know,' listening to your own truth underneath how you thought you 'should' be living, and releasing everything that is not in alignment with your personal truth, do you open a channel to your own source of vitality, peace, and connectedness that, over time, fills you completely so that you no longer need anything or anyone external to yourself for happiness.

Once you experience connection with Spirit, and feel joy arising from within you (rather than because of something external to you), you will understand that you have cultivated the beginning of a life-long relationship with yourself that is rich, deep, and nourishing. Oh, and demanding! On the spiritual path we are constantly called to look more closely into the mirror, understand our essential self more fully, and let go again and again of what no longer serves.

To start connecting with your essential self, and invite that submerged self to come up from 10-feet under water to the surface of your being—do some left-eye to left-eye gazing in the mirror. With a candle lit near the mirror, gently gaze at your left eye in the reflection for as long as you can. Blink when you need to, but return to the soft gaze. At first, this might feel very uncomfortable. Over time, you will become more at ease with yourself, and will be able to gaze for up to a half hour. Gazing in this way connects you to your soul self, and generates a deep feeling of peace and acceptance.

As you feel comfortable with the gazing practice, begin adding loving affirmations including: 'There is worth here,' 'I love you,' and 'I forgive you.' You may cry as you say these affirmations. That is perfectly fine to acknowledge and release the pent up feelings. Keep saying the affirmations until they no longer cause an emotional reaction. In this process of witnessing yourself, accepting yourself, forgiving yourself, and loving yourself—you become stronger and stronger, and sink your own roots into the ground deep and wide like an old Oak tree.

Focusing attention on 'now'

Eckhart Tolle says that we experience fear and anxiety when we are focused on the future, and sadness/anger/regret when we are focused on the past. He says that we can escape all of this by staying in the present moment with our attention. He invites you to focus your attention on this moment with the question "What is wrong in this exact moment?" More often than not, the answer will be "Nothing."

I recommend listening to *"The Power of Now"* audiobook by Eckhart Tolle to fully experience his consciousness and allow it to permeate and re-inform your consciousness. As a person who spent all of her time focused on the past and the future until a few years ago, I can very honestly vouch for the peace that comes when you can focus your attention on 'right now.'

One way to focus attention on 'now' is to turn off your primary awareness (sight) by closing your eyes, and allow other senses to inform your perception. 'See' inside of yourself with your mind's eye, and drop your inner gaze from your mind down to your heart. Look or feel around with your attention all of the areas surrounding your heart. If your attention returns to thoughts in your mind, see if you can drop your attention like an anchor lower into your being, perhaps to below your ribcage, down to your belly button, or even lower to your pelvis. Keep dropping your attention into your body whenever it pops back up into your mind. While you are focusing your attention inwards in this manner, breathe evenly in and out. You can even breathe in for a count of five, and out for a count of five. You can breathe in through your nose, and out through your mouth. These different ways of breathing are simply to occupy your mind so it will stop talking.

Once you are fully in your body, aware of your entire being, you may experience stillness in your mind that feels absolutely yummy. As with most practices, fake it until you make it and keep *practicing*.

Reclaiming self through celibacy

It had been a year and a half since the end of my marriage, and I had had a string of lovers. Each lover sent me a layer deeper into self-loathing, into the muck that was my inner shadow, into the dark recesses that desperately needed the light. I kept seeking that piece of cheese through the rat maze, imagining I had found it, raising my hope and delight with grand illusions, only to become disappointed with the truth that I eventually allowed myself to see. The final blow that knocked me down onto rock bottom was a man who I allowed to sexually dominate me, letting him prey on my desperate need for love and attention. Finally it came to light that he was married, that he had been lying to me, and my faith crumbled.

My light was fading. The darkness inside was consuming me. I knew I had to do something different. I prayed aloud to whoever might be listening, and just then I saw an invitation to a retreat with Vanessa Stone, a local spiritual leader, for the coming weekend. I knew it was synchronicity and I signed up.

Throughout the weekend of spiritual inquiry, it became clear that I was addicted to men and sex. I had learned in my life how I could gain the feelings of love and protection and acceptance through sexual intimacy. The problem was that I didn't know other ways of gaining love, protection and acceptance for myself. I was hooked on the human marketplace as the source of my self-worth and it was backfiring on me.

During a conversation with Vanessa, she set me to task: "100 days of celibacy. You will not find the deep love you seek in the human marketplace. Let God make love to you. Give God a chance." I tried to bargain down to 30 days but Vanessa laughed. "What's so hard about 100?"

So I gave myself a gift more immense than I could possibly understand at the time—I took the celibacy challenge. I visualized the 100 days of celibacy as a pyramid with 100 steps. I tasked myself to stay on each step a full day. I told myself that if I felt discomfort, I would simply witness the feeling and let it pass.

On step 6 I fell off the pyramid when one of my former lovers stopped by for coffee. I really could have gotten down on myself at this point for lacking the willpower to commit to the goal of 100 days without sex. But I gave myself another gift: compassion. I consoled myself that the climb up the 100 steps of the celibacy pyramid was the same as meditating. The practice of meditation is not to forcefully prevent thought with the notion that occurrence of thought equals failure to meditate. The practice is to observe without passing judgment or holding onto the thoughts that arise during meditation.

Similarly, the practice and intention of celibacy is to bear witness to self in reaction to this intention, in immersion with this intention; not to sit in judgment when things do not evolve as I intended. Instead I bore witness to myself, observing reaction and behavior, and renewed intention afresh. I started over at 1 and made it all the way to 100 days of celibate commitment to self.

Since this initial bout of celibacy, I have subsequently gone several months at a time (up to 8 months in one stretch) without engaging in intimacy with another person.

What I gain from celibacy is clarity. Clarity that the source of my fullness is connection to Spirit and Pachamama (Mother Earth). Clarity that my attention is better served to be focused on my spiritual development and personal growth. Clarity that the yummy experience of sexual intimacy begins with a heart-to-heart connection. Clarity to discern the quality of intimate engagement a person I meet might be capable of sharing. Clarity that love is a sensation independent from sex. Clarity that other forms of physical interaction can be fantastically wonderful, such as warm, extended hugs.

I also gain fortitude from celibacy, especially the strength to be patient until a fulfilling opportunity for conscious loving engagement unuolds in my life. The longer I engage in celibacy, in fact, the less willing I am to give it up to assuage myself during a brief moment of longing or loneliness. When I am celibate, I notice that my self-belief increases as well as my desire to give myself the gift of a loving intimate experience. Ironically, the longer I am celibate, the more attractive to men I seem to become.

My goal of celibacy, whenever I choose it, is not to spend my life without sex. My goal is to focus inwards and cultivate the internal resources that grow my unique light and power without distraction or interference from others' energetic entanglement.

If you are finding yourself in a similar relationship to sex as I experienced early in my post-divorce journey, consider taking the celibacy challenge. For 100 days, commit to yourself the time and space to gain a different perspective. The view from the top of the celibacy pyramid is a 360 degree view of YOU.

Recognizing and healing repeating patterns

If you've ever tossed a flower into a stream, only to see it suspended in place against the current by some invisible force, you have witnessed a profound insight into what happens to us when we cannot release our past, our unconscious beliefs about ourselves, the endless chatter of our 'story,' or the hook of what we believe others think of us. Life is flowing all around us, past us, effortlessly gliding on down the stream while we remain tethered in place by an invisible thread.

Alberto Villoldo, founder of the Four Winds Light Body School, says that a repeating pattern in our life begins with an original wound. That event shaped part of your belief system so profoundly that you keep manifesting the experience of it again, and again, and again. Using the energy medicine I learned at school, I help my clients shift past these repeating patterns by clearing the imprints in their energy fields that are beckoning these patterns to be manifested. I also receive energy healings from fellow graduates as I continue exploration of my own patterns.

In my life I have had confusing relationships with men where they can be very loving and kind and supportive, and then the shoe drops and they disappear or they change to abusive. Abandonment. And for most of my life I believed I must have done something wrong to make them leave me or abuse me. I know the original wound in my life was when my natural father left and I never saw him again. As a toddler, I didn't understand that it was my mother's choice to hide me from my father; I only knew that something bad happened that was my fault and then my daddy left. If you read my book, *Awakening To Me*, you'll see all the ways I have worked to shift the patterns in my life that stemmed from a tumultuous early beginning in life. *→ my mom treating me badly. I was a bad daughter*

Throughout these last years of healing and energy medicine, a lot has shifted. The relationships have improved, each time with a partner who is more available, more supportive, more loving. I have a deep awareness that these external relationships with men have reflected to me the inner state of my being as I have healed through the energy medicine. How much I loved myself on the inside was a direct reflection of the type of relationship I was experiencing with a man on the outside. Through this process I have come to understand at a deep, profound level that it was never the man 'doing' to me, it was my choice of man doing the pattern to myself. Another way of saying this is that whenever you want to blame someone else for doing something to you, re-frame it. "He ignores me" becomes "I ignore myself" or "I chose him to give myself the experience of being ignored, again." Thanks Self!

Part of what happened to my internal security system when I was just over 1 years old and lost my father, and then lived for a couple of years with an abusive step-father who tried to kill my mother in front of me, is that I developed trust issues. Surprising, I know. Not only have I had trust issues, but I have leaned towards self-doubt and confusion when faced, yet again, with my pattern. I had a very loving and supportive father from the time I was 5 years old who showed me an entirely different way to be in relationship. And I'm a pretty intelligent woman; I graduated cum laude from Smith College, an Ivy

League college for women. Still, repeating patterns set when you're a toddler are smarter than you. The mind of a toddler is a sponge—we believe everything we see and we make lots of leaps of judgment because we lack logical thinking. The inner agreements we make as toddlers create the foundation of our belief structure. My inner toddler agreements created a belief structure that automated the mechanism for having my trust issues touched and my self-doubt inflamed again, and again, and again: Pick a man who is unavailable.

Cruel, mean, critical

ignores me

belittles me

If I run down the roster, I see the pattern clearly. I spent years choosing to date men who live remote, denying myself the joy of touch (I am very tactile) and triggering my abandonment issues by selecting men who are comfortable with infrequent communication. When I requested of a man-friend that he give me a text message heads-up before going offline for 5 days (a regular occurrence), he rebuffed me as needy. When I asked if he would respond to my messages within 24 hours, he said we should be friends.

He did not abandon me. I abandoned myself by choosing to date him. The fact that I allowed myself to be romanced, and I ignored all the signs that this person was commitment-phobic—is not his fault. It's mine. Deeper into the rabbit hole, at some point I began to realize that the beacon inside of me calling to be abandoned was potentially eliciting this response from these men, who might actually behave very differently in relationships with other women. The healing is always with the Self. We are manifesting our lives in every moment based on our beliefs, and how we choose to act upon them.

So what advice do I have for getting oneself out of the repeating pattern?

- Stay the course with personal work. Especially when we are dealing with early childhood trauma, repeating patterns take time and perseverance to work through. Keep a spotlight on the places of self-deception and continue chiseling into those foundational beliefs. Energy medicine helps tremendously to shift the pattern more quickly. Don't give up on yourself.

- Keep listening to your story, and not believing it. By setting the intention of listening deeply to our inner thoughts, and paying attention to our state of 'being' when we are reacting to a situation, we invite a spotlight that illuminates the source of our invisible tether to the past and unconscious agreements and beliefs. Becoming conscious means hearing the words that you speak in your mind, the stories that you tell about yourself by rote to anyone who will listen—and simply witnessing, not **believing**. The first time you witness yourself telling a lie, and you change it by questioning the thought like a scientist would conduct an experiment, you will detach the invisible thread and begin floating down your river towards a new life of *your* choosing.

- See the light at the end of the tunnel (before you can actually see it). Maintain the awareness that an infinite number of relationship experiences are being had all over the world. If you keep having the same one over and over, that doesn't mean that all relationships around the world are exactly like yours. Being caught in a loop is frustrating, but take comfort that other possibilities DO exist.

- Take a break from dating and sex. I have purposefully gone celibate for periods of time simply to shake off the confusion and rebuild my self-esteem and inner strength. Being on the human marketplace is vulnerable and often self-defeating. Each time I have chosen celibacy, I have come back stronger and more confident with deeper self-awareness and understanding of my patterns. When you are clear and strong, it's easier to avoid unhealthy seductions (or, let them go once you spot them).

- Cultivate other support structures. It's brilliant to put your energy into friendships—they last a lifetime. Becoming an integral part of a supportive community is also wise. Maintaining connections to friends and community even once you are in a relationship is critical because it helps you stay you. And often times your close friends can spot the pattern before you can.

- Continue learning. Take personal development courses, or read books to educate yourself and shine a light on places you need to heal. Read *Attached: The New Science of Adult Attachment and How It Can Help You Find - and Keep - Love*. It's very helpful information about aspects of different relationship attachment styles that might help you decipher the codes for your own relationships. I also recommend *The Mastery of Love* by Don Miguel Ruiz and *In the Meantime* by Iyanla Vanzant.

- Know that you are worth love. Nurturing yourself reinforces the deepest truth your toddler needs to know: You are worth love. Once all aspects of you really, deeply know that you are worth love, you won't need the magical relationship to prove it. The sweep-you-off-your-feet-instant-romance is cotton candy. It's fluff. Compared to deep self-love, it is unsubstantial, fleeting, and fantasy. At its core, instant romance is a seduction. Being seduced can seem thrilling, but being loved is deeply satisfying. It's the difference between a candy bar and a five-course five-star meal. Being loved is nourishing all aspects of yourself. It's giving yourself all the support you need to grow along the soul's journey. Love is a marathon, not a sprint.

When I ended a significant relationship I believed was the love of my life, I felt frustrated. I asked my teacher "Does this work ever end? Will I ever be through the woods on this pattern? Does it ever get easier?" Her response: "The growing never stops or why would we be here? The more we see our shadow the quicker we move through these lessons until they become our strengths...the very fabric of our lives and who we are becoming."

Parenting by yourself

As my older son finished middle school, it became necessary for him to live with me full-time to reduce the conflict occurring between him and his father. Suddenly, I became his sole parent. Because of the dynamics between father and son, there were lots of small challenges that I had to manage on my own without involving my ex-husband. Many times, this felt overwhelming.

In my marriage, my ex-husband and I had opposite roles: good cop and bad cop. Guess which one I was? Well, that all worked just fine when the bad cop was around to enforce the rules. But once I had to serve both roles, things got very uncomfortable for me. I really wanted another bad cop that could do my dirty work.

In fact, one day I realized that it was this deep desire to avoid the yucky part of parenting that was causing me to become a serial dater. I wanted to find another partner to help me pay the mortgage, buy the groceries, cook dinner, and… discipline my boys. Deep in my subconscious, I was feeling helpless and wanting to be rescued.

Once my dark truth was exposed, I had to admit that there was slim to no chance of a savior riding up on a white stallion. I had to accept the full responsibility that was already mine. I had to face the aspects of myself from my childhood and teen years that held resentment for 'rules,' and step into the role of loving parent to set much-needed boundaries for my son. I had to love my son enough to do my personal work: forgive my parents for their strict parenting, release my guilt over bringing my son into a critical environment, get comfortable creating 'my' version of boundaries, and spread the news that a new 'sheriff' was in town.

With the separation into two households, you get the opportunity to heal those wounds from childhood, or perceptions about your parents, that your ex-spouse may have represented for you during the marriage. You get to claim your wholeness as a parent.

Building resiliency

Once you start down the path of spiritual development, the challenges will come. At first those challenges feel like tidal waves washing away all sense of stability and security. You can be left feeling like there is no ground beneath your feet.

When the waves start to calm down, you might think you are in the clear: only blue skies lie ahead. But this is a false hope. We are here to learn and grow, and we do so by facing and overcoming challenges.

What I have noticed about the challenges over time is that my perception is changing when the waves descend. I notice that each situation that I initially react to as a problem or loss turns out, with time and patience, to be a blessing. If I can stay as neutral as possible when the challenge arises, if I can avoid becoming attached to the outcome, if I can resist taking it personally, and if I can be patient and watchful as events unfold—then I will learn that I am observing the Universe washing away something that no longer serves me in my spiritual development.

Navigating the crashing waves takes persistent redirection of thought, loving kindness and compassion towards Self, and cultivation of a deep and abiding trust in Spirit. It also takes a willingness to look at why we feel suffering at the change before us. Is it because we fear we will lose something that we have come to rely on for our happiness? If so, this is an opportunity to cultivate this 'something' within ourselves.

For example, when a relationship ends it can be hard to face the idea of losing the feeling of being in love. It feels really wonderful to be in love. But actually, it is a false notion to think that the love came from the other person: the love came from within yourself. Moreover, you can bring up this feeling of love inside of yourself anytime you want to feel it: it can simply be the feeling without any object of affection associated with it. This feeling belongs to you. It was your experience, and it is yours to keep forever, whether the person who inspired the feeling is around or not.

Once we cultivate the ability to feed ourselves the experiences that we crave from people and things outside of ourselves, we develop resiliency towards the challenges of life. We are not at the shoreline anymore where waves are crashing down. We are further out to sea, still bobbed about by life's relentless motion, but not thrown quite so far and wide. And sometimes, we are even grateful that the wave swept away the cobwebs and washed the slate clean for new possibilities.

Encouraging the princess to become an Empress

From the time a little girl is born in Western society she is being trained how to be a princess who is rescued by the prince. Sleeping Beauty: rescued by the prince's kiss. Rapunzel: rescued by the prince who climbed the tower. The list goes on of all the fictional girl characters whose lives were made wonderful by the simple addition of a man. These princesses were perfect in every way: beautiful, kind, smart, sweet, youthful, giving, selfless, virgins. These poor defenseless pretty creatures were simply constrained by some external force from which they were powerless to break free, and they needed the prince to save them.

If no one interferes to disrupt this dangerous delusion with its messages of perfection and helplessness, then little girls grow up to be women who don't know how to handle the maturation process which includes speaking your mind, stepping into personal responsibility, and accepting the reflection of aging in your physical appearance. Acrylic nails, fitness routines to keep your booty small, liposuction, plastic surgery, botox injections to cover up the signs of aging: all designed to keep us looking like the youngest, prettiest princess so we can attract and retain the prince. Our value as women is reduced to external appearance and a soft-spoken sexy demeanor that caters to the source of our security (or what we're trained is the only source of our security)—the man. I was trapped in this princess role in my marriage, acting the part of the Playboy bunny to keep my power over my husband via sexual manipulation.

The problem with being a princess is that it denies expression of the majority of what a woman actually thinks and feels. Submerging your authentic self to play a role eventually leads to a dark place of anger, depression, sadness, or jealousy; typically following the realization that the younger princesses have you beat at looking the part. When I finally imploded and the walls of my princess prison came tumbling down, I witnessed in myself a deep underlying rage that eight months later revealed itself as an ovarian cyst the size of a Texas grapefruit. The seat of my creative powers as a woman, my womb, had taken the hit of 20 years of self-denial and I lost my right ovary.

After I left my husband, I took a hard look in the mirror and began letting go of the bullshit, and embracing the real underneath. As I shed the false masks, worked to uncover my truth, and learned how to stand in my own power, I had a lot of wobble. I became intensely aware of how popular culture—magazines, movies, media—reinforces the myth again and again that to be secure and happy you simply *must* have a man by your side and a big diamond on your finger. I had been through princess hell, and I knew I had to break out of it completely and move into a new paradigm where I was the source of my own power and truth. But I had been very efficiently trained in the couples construct whereby I was emotionally incomplete, and financially vulnerable, without a man. I was trapped in the Lovers Card.

Metaphorically speaking, the Lovers Card is only supposed to be one stop along a woman's life journey. Yet many women in our society spend their entire lives in the Lovers Card, seeking validation, love and safety from external sources and unable to tap into that deeper wellspring of love and security from the true Source. I was trapped in the Lovers Card for most of my adult life until, at 45, I was at school with the Four Winds and was given a higher perspective of a woman's life journey. This higher perspective showed me how the female moves into the Lovers Card to procreate (check), then journeys to the underworld to face shadows (check), and then returns to life as an Empress, and eventually a High Priestess. Wait a minute...I had gone through the underworld and faced my shadows, but then was trying to return to the Lovers Card. I was going *backwards* on my journey.

Ironically, at the time I was dating a man long-distance who was the epitome of romance. The seduction of juicy love messages with his deep rambling baritone London accent created the most intensely perfect fodder for my delusions and kept me trance-like in the Lovers Card. Everyone who listened to one of his messages inevitably exclaimed "I love him too! He's my soul mate!" He was *goooood*. I desperately wanted to believe that I had found my soul mate at last.

There was a moment, however, during the final class for my training with the Four Winds where I could no longer ignore the truth: I was deluding myself about this man. Through intense personal work at class it became impossible not to see the truth that this man had not worked in the entire four months I had known him, and that he had hundreds of female friends on Facebook who were no doubt sympathetic to his economic struggles. The realization hit me like a ton a bricks and my inner three year old had a fit and actually pounded the lunch table "I don't want to give him up!" I was astonished to witness myself (and thankful my classmates did not judge me for this outburst). I had been protecting myself from seeing the truth so that I could keep the illusion of my 'soul mate.' It was time to step into the Empress card, claim my own power and truth, and leave my emotional crutches behind. There was no one to rescue me. I had to rescue myself.

Leaving the Lovers Card, and stepping fully into the Empress Card, proved to be a journey that required determination, focus, and faith. To become an Empress, I had to break free of archetypal energies that run like blood through our society. The Lovers Card is not just a card in the Tarot deck, it is a force to be reckoned with energetically. Spirit was constantly testing me. I dated one man who wanted to buy me an entire bottle of wine at dinner so I could 'take it home,' and then weeks later texted me "Are you sure you're ok financially? Do you need help?" It was tempting for a second, the idea of being rescued from my financial mess, but all I needed to do was remember being a Playboy bunny in my last marriage and the answer was a resounding "No. I do not need help. Thank you."

When I discovered that my full-time employment as a technical writer was ending with a layoff (I received almost a year's notice), I was anxious about how I was going to support myself when it finished, and still live my dream of being a writer and energy healer full-time. In the back of my mind those old tapes were constantly running about how I needed to find a man quick to support me before my job ended.

Instead of listening to these messages from the ever-present Lovers Card, I invited Empress wisdom into my life. The Empress helped me see that I needed to fully face up to my financial situation and start taking actions to resolve it. Almost instantly upon making the decision to do so, a resource appeared to help me navigate these murky waters, as described in the section *Handing finances as a single parent*.

The more I witnessed and dismissed the fear-based messages of the Lovers Card, and dug deep inside for my inner Empress, the louder her voice became. She spoke of maintaining integrity, pursuing right-relationship to all the aspects of my life, being present and witnessing my actual life situation, cultivating strong faith in my own wisdom, pursuing a course of action with certainty, and taking steps to pull the resources to myself that I needed to build my life. She encouraged me to leave behind the delusion that I was a helpless princess, and embrace the real power pulsing through my veins. She invited me to connect deeply to Spirit and the Pachamama, and showed me how living as an Empress is mimicking Mother Earth and helping everything around me to grow with nurturing compassion and love. She put a mirror in front of me so that I could see I had already done the most amazing thing: I had created two incredible human beings and nurtured them nearly to the point of adulthood. Aside from this greatest accomplishment, I had successfully completed a myriad of life challenges that many people would feel daunted to even begin.

"You have already succeeded," the Empress said to me from deep within.

Living as an Empress is:

- Having complete presence with your current life situation
- Mindfully acknowledging fears and doubts and desires
- Accepting that uncertainty and experimentation are part of the journey

- Speaking your well-considered truth even if it causes an adverse reaction
- Lovingly focusing (and re-focusing) your attention on what you want to create
- Responsibly taking action to maintain integrity in a shifting world
- Collaborating with the natural forces of life to birth, nurture, and lay to rest the many aspects of our lives

It is walking in harmony with the light while honoring the shadows. It is finding within you the rich soil in which to plant new seeds. It is tapping into your intuition to know when to give birth, when to stand back and simply witness, and when to let go. Ultimately, it is being a mother and helping everything around you to flourish— including yourself.

Spreading your roots

Allowing Empress energy to permeate your life results in roots that reach deep and wide into family, friendships, and community. As I cultivated Empress energy within myself, I realized more and more the many ways I could experience love and connection beyond romantic relationship, and I found deep fulfillment from these extended relationships. I practiced the art of total presence with each person I encountered during the course of my day, and I discovered the richness that could be received from deeply giving. I regularly stepped outside of myself and the concerns and fears of my ego to listen attentively to another person, and I never failed to learn a lesson for my own life in doing so. Through the course of being a sacred witness, I deepened my faith and gained perspective of my own journey.

Discovering my purpose as an energy healer and inspirational speaker and writer also fueled my desire to help others grow as I learned new spiritual lessons of my own. Whenever I found myself feeling lack, I could easily swing into abundance by practicing prayer ceremony, leading a class, or conducting a healing session. I had found a path that helped me pull out of unhealthy mind traps, clear myself of unproductive patterns, understand my own spiritual journey, and experience deep fulfillment from helping others.

As my roots sank deeper into the Earth, I found that my relationship to dating shifted as well. I claimed the driver's seat, evaluating each new prospect as to how well his personality and life situation meshed with my own. Rather than figuring out how I could become someone who could fit into his world, or allowing myself to concoct fantasies about soul mates, I regarded him and his world with non-attachment and clarity. Instead of hauling my suitcase of needs behind me, sending off flares for the knight in shining armor to rescue me, I learned how to stay present and be a witness to the unfolding of a person with time and experience, again without attachment to the outcome. I stopped taking it personally if it didn't work out with a man I liked. I began to trust that a relationship would evolve and persist if it was for my highest good; otherwise, I would soon discover the purpose or life lesson that I was meant to experience by being in relationship with that person.

None of this is to say that my heart didn't ache whenever a relationship ended with someone I really liked. I just means that although I recognized in myself a strong desire for a love relationship, I also knew the quality of relationship I wanted to cultivate and was not willing to compromise. Also, I could readily witness that I had a very full life without a lover.

Navigating independence and relationship

Everything in life is creating right relationship between yourself and the shifting environment around you. So even as I wrote about the importance of developing a strong grounding in self with support from community and family and friends, it is also true that denying yourself the pursuit of a love relationship—if you want one—is a trap. I've come to see it as risk-avoidance; and because I understand that fear-based choices or beliefs are rooted in the wounded ego, I know that whenever a choice is coming from fear it needs to be evaluated deeply.

For a while, I found myself in relationship scenarios that essentially offered me uncommitted connection. I was having sex with a fireman who clearly stated upfront "I don't want anything even remotely resembling a relationship." So every time I would engage in intimacy with him, I would give my body specific instructions to not get attached; "Body…we are simply sharing a sexual experience with this man—absolutely no cords to this man, or him to me!" And it worked. But I felt no deep emotional connection; it was a purely physical exchange. Clean of emotional drama, but devoid of true intimacy. A part of me remained behind layers of cellophane, untouched even as my body was being ravaged.

Then I dated a man for whom I felt real attraction on all levels. He brought out the best in me; I noticed how with him I wanted to be funny and lighthearted. I felt free and enjoyed our exchanges. We had an amazing first date where we talked nonstop for almost 20 hours, enjoying each other's stories. I felt so excited about the prospect of exploring this man and how we might build something real together. And then we talked about relationships, and our current theories about them. He said, "Relationships don't last forever, they are transitory; but we try to make them permanent. Instead of just accepting that they are true in this moment, we try to make them forever, until death do us part." I found myself agreeing based on my marriage experience. I put so much effort into keeping it alive, only to have it crash and burn after 20 years of trying to hold it together; and I know that the reason it failed was because we each grew up and apart. Unavoidable. It's like the marriage convention in our society expects us to get married for life, and commit to one person for the duration; but we are not the same for our entire lives. If we're doing our personal work, we grow and change as we develop; and when we change there's a good chance we will no longer fit the mold of the marriage we agreed to back when we were that less mature, less developed version of ourselves. I've witnessed several marriages where the people in the union stagnated for fear of changing and outgrowing one another, for fear of nullifying the marriage. As a person committed to becoming the best that I can be, if it's a choice between the freedom to become who I am or saving the marriage under false pretenses—it's clear what I would choose because I did it already.

But even as I agreed to the philosophy shared by my new lover, my light grew a little dimmer. This idea that the end is coming, has actually been pinpointed at some future date and time, before the relationship even got started, caused me to momentarily lose enthusiasm for this budding romance. Why pursue something at all if you know it's going to end? How could I give myself to it knowing that the death of it had already been predicted?

This made me question many things. Knowing that every relationship is a mirror to help us understand ourselves from a new, deeper perspective, I realized there were some truths I needed to witness about myself. Had I warned other lovers I might jump ship after doing intense energy work at my school, since I knew that often I changed dramatically as a result of shedding all that no longer serves (part of what no longer serves me being the current relationship)? How fair was that to the other person? Of course, my primary mission on this planet is to improve myself and ascend spiritually; but what happens to the unfortunate fellow who stakes his fortune with mine as I grow and decide to pursue different plans? What is *ayne*, right relationship, for a conscious individual on the path of the spiritual warrior when that person is also in union with another? At what point does another person's interest become a consideration of the individual's journey?

This new lover said he wanted to pursue happiness (his own happiness) as his top priority. What is wrong with that? Who doesn't want to be happy? And as his potential partner, I wanted him to be happy; I certainly didn't want to stand in the way of someone I cared about being happy. Each of us had experienced relationships that were emotionally abusive, and I did not want to be a perpetrator of that kind of disrespect and violation of the trust. But what dawned on me was that nagging question—where do I fit into his story when he's already written me out of it? What do I do with his character in my story knowing we 'will' decide to split the script in two?

I found I needed resolution on this dilemma before I could move forward, before I could open my heart to the possibilities of all that could be experienced with this man. So I negotiated a deal. Instead of a definite future ending to our budding romance, I asked him to put a question mark, to join me in a big YES to more experiences together. He agreed with a smile. The truth was that we didn't really know what was going to happen in the story of us. We only could see a couple of steps ahead. So in a way, any kind of certain prediction of the outcome would be a lie intended to protect us from the fear of the unknown. The most authentic path I could walk was to embrace the mystery and trust that whatever evolved between us would be for my benefit.

As I renegotiated our question mark future, I had many fearful thoughts and projections and urges to run or throw it all away. The ego remembers the heartache, and does not ever want to feel it again. The ego cleverly disguises its fear-based thinking as sound logic and practicality. The way to know whether a choice you are making, or a thought you are thinking is from the soul or the ego is locate its source—is it coming from fear or love? If fear is the motivator, the choice is a strategy to avoid getting hurt. But we are not here to avoid getting hurt. We are here to love fully. Opening our hearts and choosing the path of love requires faith, trust, and giving yourself even if there is a possibility of getting hurt. The goal is not avoid experience, but to immerse in it and learn from it.

I learned during my journey that the body is an excellent sounding board for decisions. When I thought about turning away from this man, my heart ached. When I allowed the fears of my ego to dominate my thinking, my heart clenched and churned in my chest. When I returned to love, returned to trust, returned to faith—my heart glowed and I felt free and safe and protected. All is well, I realized in that moment. I chose to keep moving into the future with that uncomfortable question mark and have faith.

Shifting feelings of lack to abundance

It's important to shift feelings of lack into the realization of abundance at the moment you feel the onset of that lower vibration. When our inner state is lack we will receive situations that reinforce the feeling of lack. The more we clean and clear our inner state of heavy emotions and self-judgment, and move into peace and contentedness, we will experience situations that bring us more of the good we are feeling inside. Watch and notice your external experiences because they are a reflection of your inner state.

Shifting lack into abundance is a moment-by-moment process of being present with the current life situation, having awareness of underlying thought patterns and emotions, and doing personal spiritual work to clean and clear out whatever is no longer serving you on your journey. The Universe is paying close attention. If you say you do not want a relationship that is solely based on texting, and yet you keep texting with a person who will not move into greater forms of connection, then you will not move forward into a relationship that is in-person until you end the texting relationship.

Living as 'Me'

When I left my marriage, I was looking for the perfect partner to join in a 'We' relationship. Along my journey, I became aware that I was already complete as 'Me,' but evolving. At a certain point I realized that the 'Me' stage of life was about shedding all that was not me so that I could shine the light of my authentic self. Each layer I shed refined my perspective, my energetic vibration, my personality, and my relationship desires. During periods of intense growth and change, I came to expect many short-term relationships; the purpose of these brief connections was to catch snapshot mirror reflections of my inner evolution through the external eyes of another.

One of the roles I had to shed as part of fully embracing the 'Me' stage of life was the *Pleaser* whose job was to live for others (especially men). As a woman, I was domesticated to seek attention and validation from external sources, and then put other people's needs above my own. Starting in junior high school, I learned that the way to win a boy was to figure out what he liked and become *that* so he would like me. I wasn't supposed to appear 'needy' or call him first or tell him I liked him before he told me. I wasn't supposed to take the lead because I needed to let him do that. Essentially, as a natural born leader with a strong personality and will, I was supposed to repress myself, pretend to be something I'm not, and wait for the guy to work up the nerve. This belief system was exactly what led me to being a geisha in my marriage which generated a great deal of self-loathing. During my marriage, I remember coaching a good friend, who was equally strident and single at almost 40, that in order for her to land a guy she had to pretend to not know as much, and be softer and less capable so a guy would be interested. Thankfully she stuck to her integrity and eventually met a man who loves her for exactly who she is.

As I stepped into living for myself as the top priority, I inevitably met my mirrors: men who lived for themselves as a top priority. It really pissed me off that these guys did whatever they wanted without an iota of regard for my concerns and needs, and then expected me to hop to it when they wanted something from me. This made me feel disrespected because these men clearly did not value my time as much as they valued their own. Knowing that being triggered like this was a clear sign of personal work to be done, I explored within myself for an underlying subconscious belief. I figured out the source of the issue: I judged these men for being *selfish*, a quality that was clearly 'bad' in my internal Book of Law. Then I saw that if I was going to put my needs first, I was going to have to be selfish too. Part of being selfish, and living for yourself as a top priority, is deciding what behavior to allow in your life, and what behavior gets a person booted out. Another aspect of being selfish is not feeling bad about being the bouncer that kicks out the undesired elements. And yet another aspect of being selfish is that you no longer play 'nice'; rather, you clearly communicate your truth. Getting rid of my judgements around selfishness, and giving up on being 'nice,' allowed me to be impeccable with my word, and honor my time and resources.

101

Knowing I had everything I needed inside of 'Me' gave me the strong foundation from which to evict people: my lack of need for a 'We' allowed me to be present with what actually was in front of me, and end any drains on my resources that were unnecessary.

When dating in the 'Me' stage of life, I came to view the process as simply meeting new men and discovering what aspects of personality or situations worked for me, and what aspects I preferred not to experience. It was fun learning about a new person, how he thought about the world, agreements he made about how 'life is,' and innovative ways he found to increase happiness in his own life. Whereas in the 'man hunt' stage I was looking for an instant love connection on each new date (and disappointed if I didn't find it or couldn't force it), in the 'Me' stage I approached dates in much the same way as I do a networking meeting. I was filled with curiosity and ready to learn something new about someone I just met. If it was interesting enough, I went back for seconds.

Knowing that every phase of life has its innate specialness, I learned to enjoy my freedom and the spaciousness of life as a single person. Being single offers complete choice for how to fill your time; the longer I have been single, the more I have participated in community and built friendships that have broadened possibilities for me. As a single person, I have had the opportunity to sample across many life streams, without being sequestered in one stream with one person. Deepening connection with a single person into a life-partner situation is complex and fulfilling in a different way. The 'single' phase of life offers a diversity that has its own juicy yummy quality.

Cultivating friendships with purpose

At some point I shifted from dating to find a man for a romantic relationship, into building friendships with men and women whose company I enjoyed. With my first platonic male friendships, I felt extremely confused. The emotional intimacy I had in these friendships was even deeper than I had experienced in my marriage because the men with whom I was interacting were on a spiritual and personal development path that gave them greater awareness of their intentions, and thoughtfulness with their interpersonal agreements. The confusing part? These men didn't want to have sex with me, nor a romantic relationship. I consider myself to be a fairly sexy woman, and I'd never before met a heterosexual man who wanted to be close to me, but didn't want to have sex with me. My best friend, Marques, is a man, but he is gay; I completely understand why *he* doesn't want to have sex with me.

I began to open to the possibility of having a friendship with a man simply because I enjoyed his company, and without expectation of something *more* developing. I relaxed into the now, and stopped trying to peer into my crystal ball and predict where the relationship was going. I learned to enjoy the warm tingly happy feelings I had in certain men's company (a sensation my former self would have thought was a 'sign' that this guy was the 'one') without pushing my sexual desire into the context. The 'chemistry' energy dispersed whenever I shared long hugs with these men, allowing physical and emotional connection while dissipating the more intense feelings of sexual attraction. What I found was that the butterfly feelings — without being fueled by sex—naturally faded away after a few weeks into a more relaxed vibe that was comfortably on the friendship side of the line.

My platonic friendships with men taught me that I could have a variety of relationships to fill different desires within me. I started to deconstruct the framework of the Everything Man in favor of having greater resiliency through multiple male relationships. I decided I could accept the gift of my sexy fireman lover as a standalone offering without needing him to be the 'whole package'; what is wrong with fabulous sexual fulfillment? As a single woman, I also allowed myself to consider having other lovers if I desired to do so. Soon I was questioning the very construct of marriage—if I could have all of my needs met in a reliable way, exactly as I liked it, through multiple fulfilling relationships, why in the world would I ever choose to return to a monogamous-for-life agreement?

The old beliefs no longer made sense.

Focusing on YOU

The last stage in the journey to 'Me' is to completely immerse your focus and attention on YOU. To be 'selfish' and *unabashedly* so. To shine the light of awareness into your life with curiosity and find the places you have believed you 'should' be or act a certain way. To question every agreement you ever made to be a certain way for someone else and figure out if *you* agree with it; if not, rewrite that contract to one that makes your heart elated rather than heavy. To consider every role you ever wore to make someone else happy, figure out whether it fits *you* or not; if not, put it in a bag for Goodwill. Myself as an OT?

Cleaning out your closets and drawers of outmoded roles and limiting beliefs and agreements is essential for your inner vitality. Focusing exclusively on YOU is a stage in the process of coming fully into your own power, and it only lasts as long as you choose. Part of the process is to let go of the places you have given up your power; and since this requires taking responsibility for your choices, it mandates releasing any places you believe you are a victim and helpless. If you find yourself saying things like "I can't do it because" of some external person or situation, consider what you gain from keeping yourself locked in a state of disempowerment. Once you find the answer to this question, your power will be unleashed and available to you.

When your inner truth informs your personal choices, and you clearly express your truth and set necessary boundaries as you engage in relationships, you can show up with greater love, passion, and compassion for others. Giving is effortless when you know yourself, and your internal wellspring is full from meeting your own needs.

ભ

'Me' and 'We'

Now that I have found 'Me,' I'm never giving her up for a 'We.' The lucky individual with whom I decide to engage in a 'We' relationship will be a person that shares this perspective.

I believe it's possible to have a 'We' relationship that respects the 'Me' individuals engaged in it. I also believe it is possible to have the freedom to continue to grow and expand as a 'Me' while nourishing and honoring the 'We' relationship. Freedom in a state of interdependent connection is a product of self-awareness, personal responsibility, clear communication and conscious agreement.

I cannot speak from personal experience of a conscious 'We' relationship, but I can share a story I have heard that I love. There is a couple I know of who, when they arise each day, look at each other and ask "Do I choose to be your partner today?" Every day they give themselves the freedom to decide whether the 'We' still fits 'Me.'

I love that.

☙

About the Author

Kerri Hummingbird Sami is a soul guide, shamanic healer, award-winning author and inspirational speaker. Kerri has over 20 years of experience in leading by inspiration, and a special passion for empowering women to be the artists of their lives. She mentors women to rewrite the story of their lives through inner transformation, connection to essence, remembrance of purpose, and realignment to authenticity and truth.

She is certified in energy medicine by the Four Winds Light Body school, certified as a spiritual coach by the Artist of the Spirit Coach Training Program and HeatherAsh Amara, certified in empowerment and firewalk training by Sundoor, and certified as a Warrior Goddess Facilitator. In 2014, The Indie Spiritual Book Awards conferred the honor of "Best in Category" to *Awakening To Me: One Woman's Journey to Self Love*. Kerri lives with the love of her life, his two children, and her two teenage sons in the Austin area. She works with clients around the world, and her services are described at http://www.kerrihummingbird.com.

If you loved this book, please leave a review on the retailer's website where you purchased it. You can help other readers find this book by recommending it!

Blessings,

Other offerings by
Kerri Hummingbird Sami

Please visit your favorite book retailer to discover other books by Kerri Hummingbird Sami:

Awakening To Me: One Woman's Journey To Self Love

Goodbye SSRIs: How I went of anti-depressant and anti-anxiety medication

Please visit www.fromwetome.com for special offers related to this book.

Please visit www.kerrihummingbird.com for details on life coaching and energy healing performed by Kerri Hummingbird.

Connect with
Kerri Hummingbird Sami

I really appreciate you reading my book! Here's how you can stay in touch with me!

Follow me on Facebook: http://facebook.com/Kerri.Hummingbird

Follow me on Twitter: http://twitter.com/KerriHummingbrd

Subscribe to my YouTube channel:
http://www.youtube.com/KerriHummingbird

Follow me on Instagram: http://instagram.com/kerri.hummingbird/

Follow me on Pinterest: http://www.pinterest.com/kerrihummingbrd

Follow me on GooglePlus+:
http://plus.google.com/u/0/+KerriHummingbird/

Read my author interview:
http://www.smashwords.com/interview/klawnsby

Read my blog: http://kerrihummingbird.com/blog/

Connect on LinkedIn:
http://www.linkedin.com/in/kerrihummingbird/

Visit my website: http://www.kerrihummingbird.com